With Best Wishes
for your new Home
from
All at Binks Estate Agents.

THE CHILTERNS

• HALSGROVE DISCOVER SERIES ➤

THE CHILTERNS

JON SCOURSE

HALSGROVE

First published in Great Britain in 2013.

British Library Cataloguing-in-Publication Data
A CIP record for this title is available from the British Library

ISBN 978 0 85704 195 1

HALSGROVE
Halsgrove House,
Ryelands Industrial Estate,
Bagley Road, Wellington, Somerset TA21 9PZ
Tel: 01823 653777   Fax: 01823 216796
email: sales@halsgrove.com

Part of the Halsgrove group of companies
Information on all Halsgrove titles is available at: www.halsgrove.com

Printed in China by Everbest Printing Co Ltd

CONTENTS

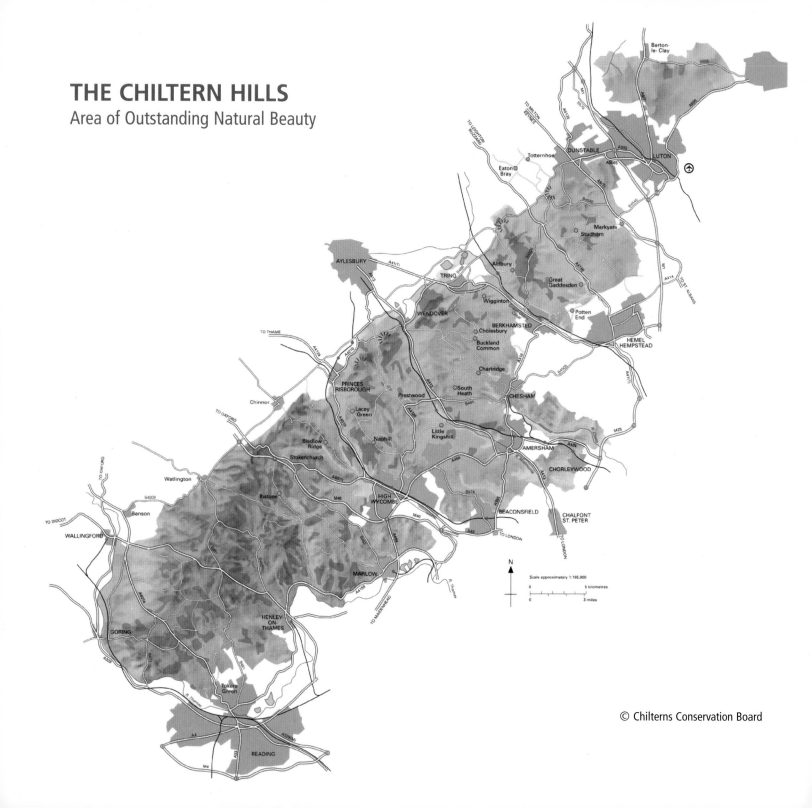

THE CHILTERN HILLS
Area of Outstanding Natural Beauty

© Chilterns Conservation Board

FOREWORD

This book is very much a personal journey to embrace what the Chilterns have offered me over thirty years, when I have lived in the area and become very attached to the chalk downs, beech woods, villages, pubs and footpaths that are the fabric of one's memories. My interest started as a keen walker, exploring the various routes, some ancient with others pioneered by the Chiltern Society and taking long days out with friends, usually with a pleasant lunch in a glorious country pub.

In more recent years I have developed my interest in landscape photography. This has prompted this book – to record visually what it is that makes the Chilterns so special. I have greatly enjoyed the challenge, especially having to explore and familiarise myself with new areas previously not known. This book is attempting to capture some of the essence of these lovely hills – the trees, valleys and wildlife.

I am greatly indebted to my wife Liz, for her support and forbearance when I was off – yet again – with my camera and spending many evenings at the computer. I would like to thank John Douglass from Goring for his advice on various photographic challenges and particularly to Roger Wyatt, a brilliant wildlife photographer who has kindly allowed me to use some of his images, especially of the red kites. This is my first effort as a writer, so I am also indebted to Fiona Danks for casting her eye over the script to ensure its accuracy as an expert on the Chilterns.

Finally, I would like to thank my dog, Eric, for his companionship in all weathers and patience on the many occasions when I was struggling over an image and he just wanted to go and catch a rabbit.

Jon Scourse

CHAPTER ONE

THE CHILTERNS – A PERSPECTIVE

The old Saxon word for chalk is chilt. It is therefore no surprise that the range of hills that flanks the Thames Valley and forms a natural barrier to the north west of London is called the Chilterns. Made almost entirely of chalk, these hills rise to 267 metres at Haddington Hill near Wendover. They form part of a very large area of chalklands that includes Salisbury Plain, the Berkshire Downs, the Isle of Wight, the North Downs and South Downs to the south and west.

Geologically, the hills form a very clear scarp from Goring-on-Thames in a south-west to north-east diagonal for nearly 50 miles, still distinct through Buckinghamshire, via

An exposure of chalk within the bank of an ancient drove near Pishill.

Right: *The view across the Vale of Aylesbury from Chinnor Hill.*

Below: *The Thames passes through a narrow cleft in the hills at Goring Gap.*

Hertfordshire and just into the Bedfordshire Downs. This helps to identify the area as a distinct feature, especially along the route of the Ridgeway long distance path. This scarp is of some interest as it has been proven that in the Pleistocene era ice did reach the northern Chilterns, with the area broadly equating to the southern boundary of the ice sheets. Even if the ice did not extend beyond Hertfordshire, the Chilterns would have been greatly affected by the intense conditions close to ice sheets that were immense in scale. The route of the Thames through the narrow "Goring Gap" is associated with the impact of the ice in diverting the previous course of the river with the formation of a lake in the Vales of Oxford and Aylesbury. These conditions probably explain the high volume of dry valleys that are of significant scale.

Chalk provides ideal conditions for the formation of flint. In the Stone Age and Neolithic periods, this was an essential raw material which would have encouraged trade along the Thames. The combination of fresh water, abundant woodlands for hunting and flint mines for tools and weapons made the Chilterns an ideal location for settlement. Defensive sites tended to be located at the ridge line, or on isolated knolls. In more recent times, flint has been an essential building material and the distinctive "brick and flint" cottages are common throughout the Chilterns.

The scarp makes a dramatic impact on the landscape. In modern times, this is most evident where the M40 motorway breaks through the hills near Stokenchurch in a vast cutting that exposes chalk strata, offering a spectacular view of the Vale of Oxford on a clear day. To the north, this scarp is very distinct in the area around Wendover and is typified by the eminence of Coombe Hill with its large monument. Further south, the hills lift sharply as the Thames edges closer to the scarp, most dramatically evident at Goring where the river passes through a very narrow valley and rises steeply on both banks.

Falling away to the south-east is a gentle slope that gradually merges into the Thames Valley and, further north, into the rolling hills in the Luton area. In fact, the lie of the land results in a close affiliation between the two areas, with the "Thames Valley and Chilterns" often being linked. However, as we shall see in this book, they are very different and the Chiltern Hiills have their own very distinct personality. As chalk is a form of limestone it is very porous, so water passes underground and there are very few streams of any significance. Water collects in underground reservoirs that emerge as springs along the lower slopes, mostly draining into the Thames. Some of these springs are significant in size, especially to the south of Wallingford where they immediately form medium sized rivers as they emerge from underground. This natural source of fresh water attracted early settlement, and in later times many water mills were built along the spring line. Today, the aquifer provides huge quantities

Elizabethan brickwork at Bix Manor.

The M40 motorway carves its way through the Chilterns near Stokenchurch.

The watercress beds at Ewelme.

The Chiltern Society is active in protecting the special qualities of the Chilterns.

Below: A replica Iron Age house at the Chiltern Open Air Museum.

The Ridgeway Path follows Grim's Ditch near Nuffield.

of water to supply the needs of the South East, most notably at Goring where there is a major underground reservoir. The water is very clean and in some places supports watercress beds, as can be seen at Ewelme. To the south, there are some fine valleys that run down to the Thames and in some places – like Hambleden – rivers form after heavy rains or in winter, but remain dry for much of the year.

Most of the Chilterns, with the exception of the more built up areas, lie with the Area of Outstanding Natural Beauty (AONB), designated in 1965 and covering 833 square kilometres. It extends from the Bedfordshire hills south of Luton, with a small outlier of the Galley and Warden Hills between Luton and Hitchin, to the Thames at Goring in the south-west. The AONB designation has given a real sense of identity to the Chilterns and is keenly supported by the very active Chiltern Society. As a consequence there is a wonderful network of footpaths and cycle routes. For any visitor, a visit to the AONB and Chiltern Society websites will provide the very latest information and details of events.

There is much evidence of occupation throughout the Chilterns. Neolithic man certainly occupied the lower levels, with evidence from the Thames floodplain of flint axes and arrowheads. Around 2000BC the Beaker people arrived from Europe and, in addition to the spectacular Silchester Hill in Wiltshire, they settled in the Chilterns area with evidence of settlements at Coombe Hill and other sites. As many of these sites are above the floodplain but below the Chiltern scarp, it is believed that the river was a major conduit for trade even in pre-historic times. In fact these were perfect conditions for early settlement, providing fresh water, good hunting in the forests with the added economic power of trading with flint.

Hill forts of Iron Age origin are found along the scarp, and in places such as Chinnor Hill and Monks Risborough there are barrows. Grim's Ditch demonstrates just how insecure life must have been in 300BC, this being a major boundary between two warring tribes, with high banks and ditches. These can still be seen very well on the Ridgeway path at Nuffield, near Wallingford.

The Ridgeway on Ivinghoe Beacon, probably used for 5000 years.

Today, there are distinct echoes of this period as two very ancient footpaths cross the Chilterns. The Ridgeway is believed to be the oldest known road in Britain, in use for at least 5000 years, once stretching from the Dorset coast to the Wash. It provided a route over higher ground for drovers, traders and invaders, less wooded, drier and more secure from attacks. New Stone Age man has left burial barrows along the length of the path. Some hill forts were also built in the Iron Age from 500BC until the Roman invasion in 43AD. The route was also witness to the conflicts between the Saxons and Viking invaders battling for control over Wessex. In later medieval times, the route was defined by drovers driving livestock from the West Country to the eastern counties. In the Chilterns, the route broadly follows the scarp from Goring to its current terminus at Ivinghoe Beacon near Tring.

The Icknield Way also claims great antiquity. Known to be a major route before the Romans, much of the route can still be traced as far as the east coast. In the Chilterns, the route is less well known than the Ridgeway and shares the same path in some places. Dating from at least the Iron Age, the route stretches from Berkshire through Oxfordshire to cross the Thames at Cholsey. Evidence from records in 1130 suggest that this route was equal in importance to the better known Fosse Way and Watling Street – the early equivalent of our motorways.

The Roman occupation was to change the lives of people in the Chilterns. With major sites at St Albans (Verulamium) and Dorchester, with Silchester also nearby, the native population appear to have been assimilated through trade and better agriculture to emerge as Romano British. Most of the evidence points to settlements being around the Chilterns rather than

Hambleden Village.

The view from Beacon Hill, looking towards Oxford across the site of Cymbeline's Castle.

Below: *The Norman church at North Stoke.*

The Old School built at Ewelme in the Elizabethan period.

within the hills themselves, although there are various small villas such as that at Downey Common near High Wycombe. Conflict came in 60/61AD with the uprising by Boudica, when many small settlements were sacked. In the southern Chilterns, there are traces of Roman roads and agricultural terraces still evident today. At Hambleden, recent archaeological digs have unearthed sinister evidence of 97 infant burials close to a major settlement, with experts concluding that this may be the site of a brothel where unwanted infants were dispatched.

As the Romans declined, so the Saxons began their invasions and by 491 they had reached the Chilterns. Many Chiltern towns now have names of Saxon origin, such as Tring and Watlington. This was a period of conflict with the Wessex tribes and no doubt there were regular skirmishes to the west of the Chilterns as Arthur rallied his forces. Many of the hills are now called "beacons" which refer to lookout positions during the raids by the Vikings who sacking nearby Reading in 871.

The Normans secured this area at a surprisingly early stage after the invasion of 1066. William the Conqueror marched his army from Kent to cross the river Thames at the first available fording point at Wallingford, then marching over the Chilterns to take London from the rear. This led to the routing of the Saxon culture, with the imposition of Norman churches and the new economic order based on the manor house. Throughout the Chilterns are many churches that were obviously Saxon in origin but were partly destroyed to make way for the new culture.

In later medieval times, the area developed in importance with the establishment of a wealthy economy based on wool. However, life could still be insecure and there are examples of motte and bailey settlements, one of the best being Cymbelines Castle near Great Kimble. The nearby Wallingford Castle, flattened later by Cromwell, was of both political and economic importance as the base for Queen Matilda in her battles with her cousin King Stephen. As a result, villages such as Ewelme are rich in medieval buildings, in that case with links to the Chaucer family.

In the eighteenth century, the area's proximity to London began to have an impact. Contact between London to Oxford and beyond demanded routes through the Chilterns. Toll roads developed for stagecoaches, evidenced by the very high proportion of obvious toll houses in many villages across the hills. Some towns also became known for stabling and accommodation, such as Nettlebed and Watlington. This was also the period for the highwayman, with local tradition that Dick Turpin frequently robbed the roads throughout the area.

Water supply was a challenge in the higher areas. Far away from the spring line of the scarp, there were a few rivers but in the uplands there was no easy supply. New technology enabled the sinking of deep wells to provide fresh water and many of these wells survive, usually at the focal point. One of the most notable is the ornate Maharajah's Well at Stoke Row.

Many of the older country land holdings like Stonor became the basis for the Victorians to create great country estates, accessible to London and able to accommodate large weekend parties for the newly settled shooting and hunting operations. In particular, the Rothschild family settled around Tring and had a long term influence in the area. At Ashridge, the Egerton family built a magnificent estate that is now used as a management college, as is the W. H. Smith family home on the Thames at Greenlands near Henley. At Nettlebed, the Fleming family established a large estate where the writer Ian Fleming was brought up. These are just a few of the very many estates that grace the Chiltern valleys to this day.

Many of these properties are more popular than ever today, offering havens for the very wealthy that are close to Town and encouraging visitors when open to the public, either as private ventures or under the auspices of the National Trust. Being near London, these estates

An example of a typical Chiltern toll-house at the Chiltern Open Air Museum.

The beautiful setting of Stonor House.

Parkland surrounds the valley at Swyncombe House.

Below: *A lock on the Grand Union Canal at Tring.*

also offer the country home for the Prime Minister at Chequers, near Wendover and the Foreign Secretary at Dorney Wood near Burnham Beeches to the south.

The impact of the Victorians was also economic. The Grand Junction Canal was built through the Chilterns, to link the Thames with the canal networks into the Midlands, providing new sources of work. The need for a comprehensive rail network forced new routes through the barrier of these hills; the first long distance railway in the world opened in 1837 between London and Birmingham passing through Tring and Amersham. Another route was to Aylesbury through the narrow valleys from High Wycombe to Princes Risborough. These routes in turn opened up the scope for more industry, with mining and quarrying using branch lines. The furniture industry, based on the steady supply of planted beech wood, prospered and made High Wycombe a major centre, reaching markets throughout the Empire.

Agriculture and forestry also prospered, with new communications opening up the expanding market in London. Most of the towns had a cattle market and in the higher villages the supply and preparation of timber for the furniture factories provided extra employment.

On the scarp near the Thames, the farms developed on a strip basis from the river and upwards to the top of the hills, enabling mixed farms to operate with cattle in the valleys, arable fields on the middle heights with sheep grazing on the chalk downlands above. A few of these farms still survive on the same basic layout.

The furniture industry has had a beneficial impact to this day. The southern Chilterns have one of the highest densities of mixed woodland in England, blessed with large swathes of wonderful beech woods that now provide leisure access as well as maintaining a commercial timber industry. Many of these woods provide a magnificent display every May with bluebells in abundance.

The Chilterns today remain a beautiful and accessible area to explore. There are of course the usual pressures to contend with, notably to protect the environment from further development. As a natural barrier between the Midlands and London, there has always been an issue with communication links. The need for a motorway resulted in the M40 in the mid-1970s, forging its way across the hills to eventually break through to the Vale of Oxford with the highly controversial cutting near Stokenchurch. This is a paradox as it does relieve the Chilterns of a vast amount of traffic and potential congestion, but is a blot on the landscape. The new HS2 high speed rail link to Birmingham is even more contentious, threatening to damage some of the best Chiltern landscapes and is being bitterly opposed at the time of the Government decision to proceed with the project.

Arable and sheep farming mix with extensive beech woods at Ipsden.

Left: *Bluebells in May are spectacular across the entire Chilterns.*

Below: *Poppies with the Chiltern scarp in the background.*

Protests tried to prevent the HS2 high speed train project through the Misbourne Valley.

The Chiltern line passing through beech woods near Little Missenden.

Right: *The New Years Day shoot at Nettlebed.*

The economy is still influenced by communications and accessibility to London. The M40 has enabled daily commuting from leafy properties in the Chilterns, as well as opening up the Midlands as a place to work. Weekend retreats are also popular, sometimes at a cost to local communities. Large estates remain popular for the super-rich, with shooting in the winter months. Throughout these hills there are very substantial country houses that offer privacy and solitude, within an hour from the City. The late John Mortimer, with his book *A Voyage Around My Father*, was a typical example of this lifestyle from his home at Turville Heath. Good rail links have also made it possible for the middle classes to settle, commuting daily from modest homes or newly built developments. As a result, service industries have grown while the more traditional industries have fallen into decline. The global trend towards cheap labour overseas has hit the furniture industry badly and the scope of the manufacturing base is greatly reduced today.

Employment today lies with light industry, specialising in information technology and light engineering operating through small industrial estates. Science and technology are important, with easy access to the intellectual wealth of Oxford, the M40 corridor and Heathrow airport.

Leisure and tourism are developing and now contribute £900m to the local economy. Most towns have a Tourist Information Centre. The emergence of walking and cycling – in particular

Autumn display in beechwoods near Goring Heath.

Aldbury – the location for several Midsomer murders.

Below: *The windmill above Turville, used for* Chitty Chitty Bang Bang.

the long-distance trails – has resulted in an increasing number of visitors from around the world. Another impact has been the emergence of television as an influence for visitors – Agatha Christie mysteries, *Inspector Morse* and *Midsomer Murders* all coalesce into this archetypal, sleepy English amalgam of murders and churchbells that is exported throughout the world. Today we have special trails to visit "Midsomer Country" which bring many visitors. The irony with this is the image it conveys of the Chilterns as having the highest murder rate in the world!

The area is also very popular as a set for films – being close to the studios in London and easily accessible. The village of Hambleden is so popular it has become a source of income for the local community, with many famous films and well known TV series being filmed in and around the area of the church. Nearby Turville was used for the *Vicar of Dibley* and the windmill above was featured in the film *Chitty Chitty Bang Bang*.

Another reason for visiting the Chilterns is the wildlife. When watching a red kite soaring nearby, it is easy to forget how near this is to London. These magnificent birds, re-introduced in the 1990s, have been highly successful, to the extent that they are now common throughout the entire area. By 2010, the conservative estimate was 1000 breeding pairs; they are rapidly expanding from their Chiltern homeland into the surrounding counties and have even been sighted over London. They can often be seen beside the M40 between High Wycombe and Stokenchurch, giving just a glimpse of what can be found deeper in the woods away from the noise. They are remarkably unflustered by human contact and seem to be very relaxed, often soaring only feet above with their very distinctive whistling calls, giving some really close up views of their beautiful colouring. Studies of their habits have discovered that these birds are great collectors, and nests have been found with teddy bears, toys from gardens and even a £10

Red Kites are now very common and spectacular to watch.

(photos by Roger Wyatt)

note. Paradoxically, the re-introduction has perhaps been too successful, as red kites have almost become a pest in some parts, with reports of unwelcome close encounters when the birds might try to steal food by swooping down on an unsuspecting victim. Some local people are feeding the kites which encourages some dependency and the RSPB is keen to discourage this practice.

The bird life is varied but the red kite is undoubtedly the local hero. Buzzards, owls and sparrow hawks are common and there are occasional merlins on migration in the autumn. Little egrets are now colonising and can be seen in the Chess Valley. Although declining, cuckoos can still be heard in spring and lapwings are hanging on when the local farmers are considerate. There are some special sites for birds, notably on the reservoirs near Tring and the local Wildlfe Trusts Warburg Reserve at Bix.

Deer – roe, fallow and the introduced muntjac – are all common and increasing, with the beech woodlands providing excellent cover. An extraordinary wildlife story are the wallabies of the Chilterns, first reported in the late 1990s and now commonly reported around Henley-on-Thames and Stokenchurch. These are thought to have escaped from a private collection or small zoo at some stage and have since become established. Rarely sighted, they live deep in

Tawny Owl.
(photo by Roger Wyatt)

Roe deer are common, especially at Ashridge.

Below: *Sunlight streams through the woods near Ashridge House.*

the beechwoods and most of the evidence is from road kill. I once saw a wallaby after a rather liquid pub lunch on a remote walk and was greatly relieved when my walking companion volunteered that he thought he might have been hallucinating!

This book breaks the Chilterns into sections in an effort to make it more logical. This is by its nature artificial. The Chiltern Hills are an exceptional area of England and wherever you visit you will find rolling hills, wooded valleys and exceptional brick and flint villages, hopefully with a beautiful pub for lunch before a walk along a footpath that was probably also an ancient route. The title of the regular magazine of the Chiltern Society is most apt – *Chalk and Trees*.

Perhaps one of the more eloquent descriptions comes from John Cowper, the eighteenth century poet born at Berkamstead, writing of the Chilterns:

There was neither tree nor gate nor style in all that country to which I did not feel a relation … I sighed a long adieu to fields and woods from which I thought I should never be parted, and was at no time so sensible of their beauties as when I left them behind, to return no more'.

Opposite: *Winter mist casts an eerie light in the beechwoods at Princes Risborough.*

Below: *Looking up at the Chilterns scarp near Shirburn.*

Exploring in the Chilterns

The Chilterns offer a great opportunity to explore a quintessentially English landscape that is very close to London. As a result the motorway links are good, with the M4 allowing access into South Oxfordshire, the M40 driving deep into the Chilterns, linking the A41 to the north with the M25. Once away from these roads, the red kites will foretell a quieter pace of life with small lanes bordered by deep beech hedges, wonderful woods and beautiful villages, most with a pub and a church. It is quite possible to just meander off the beaten track to stumble across country houses and sudden views across the valleys.

Although convenient, the car is not always the best way to explore. Far more can be seen by going slowly, by bike or on foot. There are many bridleways which are accessible for bikes (although mountain bikes are essential) with the more formal routes for longer tours. The Chilterns Cycleway is a 170 mile circular route passing right around the

Winter in the woods at Nettlebed.

22

Chilterns Area of Outstanding Natural Beauty. Over 95% of the route is on-road (mostly following minor roads), with just a few sections following towpaths, surfaced cycle lanes and bridleways.

With the leadership of the Chiltern Society, walking routes abound and the level of access is very good compared to many areas of the country. Most of the woodlands are accessible and many are well managed, such as the Wendover Woods complex, although these can get more crowded. The better solution is to purchase one of the many walking guides available through local book shops and the tourist offices, or one of the excellent guides published by the Chiltern Society. In general, the paths are quite good but do get very muddy after rain and in winter, so walking boots are advised. In addition there are the designated Long Distance paths, well documented with numerous guides. Few comparable areas have such a richness of these paths – The Ridgeway, The Ickneild Way, The Swans Way, The Chiltern Way and many more. It is always advisable to purchase the local Ordnance Survey maps as well, as they give a good feel for the landscape, its hills, woods and valleys.

Opposite: *The lanes near Turville in autumn.*

Below: *The Bull and Butcher pub at Turville.*

The Chilterns Cycleway at Aldbury.

Left: *An upturned tree exposes the shallow chalk subsoil.*

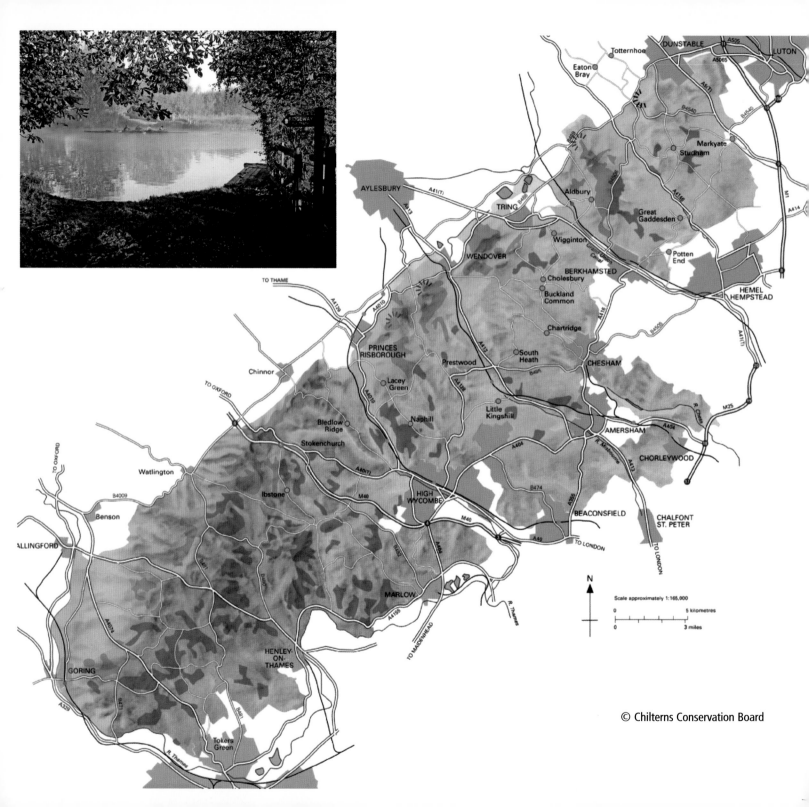

© Chilterns Conservation Board

N

Scale approximately 1:165,000

0 ————— 5 kilometres
0 ————— 3 miles

DUNSTABLE
LUTON
Totternhoe
Eaton Bray
Markyate
Studham
AYLESBURY
TRING
Aldbury
Great Gaddesden
Wigginton
BERKHAMSTED
Cholesbury
Potten End
Buckland Common
HEMEL HEMPSTEAD
WENDOVER
Chartridge
TO THAME
South Heath
CHESHAM
PRINCES RISBOROUGH
Prestwood
Chinnor
Lacey Green
TO OXFORD
Little Kingshill
Naphill
Bledlow Ridge
AMERSHAM
CHORLEYWOOD
Watlington
Stokenchurch
TO OXFORD
Ibstone
M40
HIGH WYCOMBE
Benson
BEACONSFIELD
CHALFONT ST. PETER
WALLINGFORD
M40
TO LONDON
TO LONDON
MARLOW
R. Thames
TO MAIDENHEAD
HENLEY-ON-THAMES
GORING
Tokers Green
R. Thames

CHAPTER TWO

FOLLOWING THE RIDGEWAY

This chapter follows the natural scarp defined by the geological framework of the Chilterns, where the hills drop suddenly down into the former glacial lake that is now the Vale of Aylesbury, the Vale of Oxford and finally the Goring Gap. This follows a generally clear ridge running consistently from the south-west at Goring-on-Thames, in a north-easterly direction as far as Ivinghoe Beacon and some way beyond towards Luton. Our exploration of the Chilterns commences where the Ridgeway crosses the Thames at Goring and continues towards its terminus at Ivinghoe Beacon. This ancient path also followed the scarp line, probably as its height above the surrounding landscape offered some protection and water was readily accessible from the many springs that emerge from the slopes. There are also many ancient settlements along this route, no doubt offering places to stop and trade. So, in general, our route follows that of the Ridgeway.

Lardon Chase rises behind the Thames at Goring.

Opposite: *The main line railway passes through the Goring Gap.*

The first community in this chapter following the Ridgeway is where the Chilterns really do meet the Thames at Goring-on-Thames. Here we have a famous geological feature – the Goring Gap – where the Thames courses through a narrow gap between the Berkshire Downs to the west and the Chilterns to the east. To see this really well, take a walk to The Holies, high above Streatley-on-Thames on the Berkshire bank. This is a National Trust woodland, where the path will take you to an vantage point high above the river and with Goring tucked in between the hills beside the river. From this eagle's nest, one can see the boats plying down the Thames into the locks, the beautiful church and even the cars crossing the bridge below. Occasionally, one will hear the sound of the next high speed train surging from London towards the West Country and then see it as it streams through a cutting above the village. This is Brunel's Great Western Railway, with two famous bridges that are still providing great service. The first of these is at Gatehampton, just south of Goring and the other is a few miles further north at Moulsford, near South Stoke. This superb bridge built in 1838, right on the Ridgeway, has complex brick work that is a testament to the quality and vision of Brunel's engineering skill.

When parking at the National Trust car park for The Holies, there is an equally spectacular

Moulsford Bridge, built by Brunel in 1838 and still used on one of the busiest lines in the United Kingdom.

The Thames from The Holies, high above Goring.

Right: *Early mist in winter during sunrise at the Goring Gap.*

walk across the rolling downland known as Lardon Chase. This wonderful short walk takes you to another vantage point above the Goring Gap. From here, one can get a real feel for the impact of the landscape on the routes from London to the west. Road and rail links are squeezed cheek by jowl with the beautiful, winding Thames in a glorious valley. When the mist sits in the river in the autumn mornings, there is an almost ethereal feel to the view from the top of Lardon Chase, with the church tower poking above the white layer of mist and the Chilterns beyond. This is also a good spot for an anticipatory view of the Chilterns and the journey taken in this chapter. One can see the scarp tailing away to the north-east towards Watlington, with the beech woods and chalk grassland meadows on the other side of the valley. All this makes for a wonderful setting for Goring.

Goring is a very lively village. Although popular as a retirement area, it also attracts commuters as the rail links to London are very good with regular trains making the journey in less than one hour. There is strong community cohesion and a pioneering spirit to develop new initiatives – at the time of writing discussions are under way to install a water turbine at the Goring Lock to reduce the village's carbon footprint. As with so many of these Thames settlements, there is evidence back to the Iron Age, with a strong Roman presence later on. Its physical situation, commanding the communication networks, would have made it an important strategic asset and there is evidence that this was an area for conflict between the Saxons and Vikings. The remains of a Saxon warrior, with his full set of weapons, have been uncovered within the churchyard.

A later conflict came with the Norman invasion. Originally a Saxon stronghold, Goring succumbed to the Normans and became an important centre for Robert d'Oilly, who also built Oxford Castle and was a staunch supporter of William the Conqueror. The font in the parish church is of Norman origin.

In the twelfth century there was an active chalk quarry at Hartslock, just south of Goring and still visible on the Thames Path. The stone was easily transported on the Thames and was used to build much of Reading Abbey, Wallingford Castle and Oxford Castle. Local folklore suggests that many of the archers that went to Agincourt in 1415 were trained at Goring.

The very first "flashlocks" began to appear in the sixteenth century in many places along the Thames. These comprised a single gate in a weir, which was opened to allow boats to pass through using the fast current – upstream boats were winched through. Such a lock existed at Goring and further upstream at Cleeve – both sites now being major locks and well worth a

Goring Lock – once a flashlock and scene of a great disaster.

(photo by John Douglass)

Poppies in the evening near Woodcote create an almost Italian vista.

visit, especially in summer when they can be colourful, both in terms of the language being used by stressed boat owners and with the boats themselves. Before the bridges were built, ferries linked Goring and Streatley. In 1647 there was a major disaster when the ferry went too close to the weir and capsized, causing sixty people to drown. Most were from Streatley and returning from the All Saints feast in Goring. The impact of this disaster on the local community must have been enormous, considering the population at that period would have been only a few hundred. The first proper bridge was built in 1837 at the astronomical cost of £6000, a huge amount in those days, operating as a toll bridge. The current bridge, which has to be walked to be fully appreciated, was built in 1923. The views from here are lovely, with glimpses of the river and its life, the waterfowl around the locks.

The coming of the railway in 1840 had an enormous impact. Until then, Streatley was the larger and more important village, benefiting from the road tolls from the main route between Oxford and Reading. This changed when Brunel built the Great Western Railway through the Goring Gap, with a halt at Goring. This brought much more wealth and speedy access, even in those days, to Reading and London.

Goring has attracted many well-known residents, including Oscar Wilde and Sir Arthur (Bomber) Harris – and more recently, the pop star George Michael lives here for much of the time.

Travelling north, the first village after Goring lies at a much higher altitude, almost on the plateau at 600' above sea level. Woodcote is an amalgamation of modern housing around an earlier village centre, within easy reach of Reading along the A4074 road. This has resulted in a larger than expected community compared to the surrounding villages. Perched above the surrounding countryside, there are spectacular views across the rolling landscape towards the

Patchwork fields in early summer near Ipsden.

ever present Didcot Power Station. The original Woodcote House is now the Oratory School, one of the few independent Catholic boarding schools in England. The village has a strong reputation for its community spirit, with a tradition for awards for its "best kept village" status. It also hosts one of the larger steam fairs every summer.

It should be noted that the farms that were located between the Thames and Chilterns scarp adopted a common pattern of mixed farming. This involved pasture for cattle on the river meadows, changing to arable on the drier chalk soils at a higher altitude as the land rises towards the hills, then becoming suitable for sheep grazing on the upper pastures, leading to beech woods at the highest levels. Farms therefore developed along linear boundaries from the river all the way to the ridge, a distance of several miles. To this day, there are farms at Crowmarsh and Ipsden that still work to these boundaries although the land use is now primarily arable, with occasional sheep. Cattle grazing is fairly uncommon, while outdoor pig farming has become more popular.

Nearby are smaller settlements with a totally different feel – up in the hills, such as Ipsden. This scattered village of farming activity is set in stunning surroundings. The best way to sample this is to take a drink at the King William pub at the nearby hamlet of Hailey and just take in the views of rolling hills and woods. An added bonus is the sheer number of red kites in this area. It is not unusual to see several of these huge birds at once, wheeling and turning on the wind. Beside the small church, lying south of the village, is a good example of one the many old wells that were sunk in Victorian times to overcome the problems of water supply. Although no longer in use, the ornate ironwork by a local company, Wilders of Wallingford is worth the visit.

Early settlements followed the springline, and such villages continue all the way along the scarp. Small hamlets such as Mongewell and North Stoke developed where large springs enabled mills to operate, but with the added benefit of having direct access to the Thames itself. Nearby, towards Nuffield, the Ridgeway follows the ancient Grim's Ditch with evident earthworks on a massive scale to mark this early boundary between warring tribes in the dark ages. From now on, the Ridgeway turns its back on the Thames and climbs into the Chilterns.

Staying on the Ridgeway, Nuffield lies close to the main A4130 road between Oxford and Henley. The National Trust has recently acquired Nuffield Place, which was the home of Lord Nuffield, formerly Alfred Morris. As one of the wealthiest men in England in the 1930s, he was visited here by Churchill who was seeking funding to assist the war effort in 1940. The house, which is unexpectedly modest, was bequeathed to Nuffield College Oxford with instructions that it be preserved in its original condition, with its 1950s' style of furniture and fittings. It is a fascinating place to visit, a time warp, with bakelite fittings and original versions of the earliest televisions, and old telephones without any dialling facility with twisted cord cabling. The kitchen also has a wonderful collection of tins and bottles from a

Opposite: Mixed farming and woodland on the slopes of the Chiltern scarp at Ipsden.

The spring at North Stoke supports a substantial stream that flows into the Thames.

The ancient village of Ewelme nestles in its own small valley.

past age that strikes a chord for those brought up in the immediate post war period. Despite his enormous wealth, Morris was still considered to be a "tradesman" as he started from very humble beginnings and was not easily accepted into the local society around Henley.

Ewelme is a gem, pronounced "you-elm". Another spring-line village, it boasts every style of architecture from the Elizabethan, through Georgian and Victorian to the twentieth century – and all charming. It is no surprise that there is also a village pond, watercress beds, a thatched village hall and a community shop. The crowning glory is the magnificent St Mary's church, with its unusual rood screen and one of the finest medieval tombs in England. As if this is not enough for such a small place, there are also the Almshouses, nestling almost underneath the church tower and still used for eight residents.

To visit Ewelme, it's better to get away from your car. Start at the Elizabethan School, with a path leading into a charming formal garden which in turn leads into the Almshouses courtyard. One can almost imagine this as the backdrop for a Shakespearian play – medieval timbers with fine carvings, beautiful stonework with well-kept gardens. From here, take the steps directly into the church – and there, immediately as you enter, is the most wonderful stained glass window in the chancel. The highlight of this very fine church is the tomb of Thomas Chaucer and Alice de la Pole, the Duchess of Suffolk, and the grand-daughter of

Geoffrey Chaucer. She had great influence locally, married several times and was a guardian of Margaret of Anjou at Wallingford Castle in 1472. Her will is displayed behind glass within the church vestry, which is not usually open but can be if you are lucky enough to find someone with the key. Her tomb is extraordinary, with its alabaster effigy exuding her strong personality, in contrast to the matching effigy of her own cadaver lying directly underneath in the same position. The entire tomb, with its fine carvings and gilt still shining, is so exquisite that it is believed to have been carved by the same Italian craftsmen who created the tomb of Henry VII in Westminster Abbey.

Before leaving the church, take a look around the churchyard and you will find the grave of Jerome K. Jerome, the author of *Three Men in a Boat*, who retired to Ewelme. The church is just as magnificent from the outside, standing on a slight incline but elevated above the village, surrounded by beautiful houses.

Now walk into the village, down to the pond and the village store, run by the local community and manned by volunteers. Quiet lanes lead off to elegant homes, with a lively stream running beside the main street. This leads down to a unique feature, the extensive series of watercress beds. Once commercial, these are now looked after by the Chiltern Society with local volunteers and a new visitor centre funded through lottery grants. The beds extend for about half a mile and are open during the summer months on Sunday afternoons, when guided tours are offered. It's easy to see how this was once a thriving local business, even supplying Covent Garden before increased competition forced its closure.

The setting of Ewelme completes this perfection. It nestles under rolling chalk hills that form the lower elements of the scarp, with the fine Ewelme Court high above the village, looking out across the Thames Valley. It's worth walking the Ridgeway to nearby Swyncombe to see at first hand the beauty of these folded hills, with their beechwoods.

The modern world does intervene as the largest helicopter airbase in the UK is only a mile from Ewelme at Benson. As well as being the primary helicopter base for the Royal Air

Beautiful gardens surround the almshouses and church at Ewelme.

Below: *The tomb of Thomas Chaucer and Alice de la Pole in Ewelme church.*

The watercress beds at Ewelme.

Above: *Fields in summer near Swyncombe.*

Below: *An ancient beech tree at Swyncombe.*

Fine timberwork in the almshouses at Ewelme.

Force, the airfield also hosts numerous police and air ambulance helicopters. It is not surprising that the sound of spinning rotors is never far away.

Not far from Ewelme is the site of the Battle of Chalgrove which took place in June 1643. With the Royalist strongholds in Oxford and Wallingford and the Parliamentarians centred on London, the entire Chilterns area was a front line. Skirmishes were common, especially along the settlements of the scarp. Just before the Battle of Chalgrove Field Prince Rupert led a Royalist army of 1800 to rout the Parliamentarian's garrison at Princes Risborough on 18 June 1643, taking 120 prisoners. This led to a subsequent chase by a Parliamentarian rearguard resulting in the battle on the same day.

In this particular exchange the Royalists led by Prince Rupert, nephew of Charles I, prevailed. John Hampden commanded the Parliamentarians and was mortally wounded, dying at Thame six days later. This episode is commemorated at a memorial known as the John Hampden monument just south of Chalgrove on the site of the battle.

Wallingford is just a few miles away. Although definitely not a Chiltern town, the Chilterns have had an enormous influence on its historical development. It is rarely appreciated just how important Wallingford once was, with one of the great English castles to compare with Windsor in its scale. The remains testify to the complete destruction by Cromwell, the price paid for its loyalty to the Royalist cause. The Normans occupied a town made very important in Saxon times, primarily because it had one of the very few medieval bridges across the Thames. In modern times, Wallingford owed much of its wealth to its proximity to the early farmers of the Chilterns, creating regular markets and supporting agricultural enterprises. The agricultural pioneer Jethro Tull lived at Crowmarsh, just across the river. He perfected the horse-drawn seed drill in 1701, a revolutionary invention for its time.

From Wallingford, the atmosphere changes as the Chilterns become ever more distant from the River Thames. The River Thame, a major tributary of the Thames, drains this land and meets the main river at Dorchester-on-Thames. The gap between the Thames and the scarp widens as one travels northwards, until the river swings west and becomes just a distant feature.

In the hills above Ewelme lies the hamlet of Swyncombe. Any visitors in the area in February should make sure that they visit the church of St Botolph's to see the wonderful display of snowdrops and aconites, which have become a local attraction at the annual Snowdrop Sundays every February with events in the church and teas – it's a mark that winter is at last ending with the emergence of such a delicate swathe of white in the churchyard. The Ridgeway Path passes this unusual church. Although built by the Normans, its simplicity suggests an earlier Saxon provenance, built of traditional flint and stone and without a tower. The name derives from ancient English, meaning a valley where there are wild boar. Today, this valley is one of the most perfect vistas to be found in the Chilterns. Stand beside the lane

Volunteers support the local community store and café at Ewelme.

The ancient St Botolph's church at Swyncombe.

Opposite: Wallingford was once of national importance with its castle and river crossing.

above the church and the rolling parkland of Swyncombe House is stunning, criss-crossed by inviting footpaths. The house was built in the 1840s but replaced an earlier manor house that had very close links to the church.

Watlington is a fine example of an ancient Chiltern town, one of the oldest towns in England. As with so many of the spring line settlements, there is a long history of occupation. Being on the Icknield Way, it was a good place for trading with a ready supply of water. The name itself is of Saxon derivation and the charter was granted in the ninth century, with reference to eight mansions. By the time of the Domesday Book (1086) there was evidence of a street plan which is reinforced in later medieval documents, with reference to a thriving market.

The snowdrops at Swyncombe are a local event every February.

Following the trend for chalk features in the hillsides, in the late eighteenth century an eccentric local squire decided that Watlington church would look better, when viewed from his home, with a spire. So a suitably shaped triangle (36' wide at its base and over 200' long) was scraped in the chalk in exactly the position to look like the spire for the church. This landmark still survives today.

In Victorian times, a new Town Hall was built on the site of a school, originally built in 1665. An attractive building, it stands rather awkwardly at the junction of several roads and

The chalk mark at Watlington Hill.

The Town Hall sits astride the centre of Watlington, one of the oldest towns in England.

Opposite: *Red kites often provide spectacular flying displays.*
(photo by Roger Wyatt)

as a result Watlington can be highly congested. Being so near the M40, it provides easy access for locals wishing to get to the motorway, but the narrow streets were not designed for such a heavy load of traffic and this does spoil the town centre. However, there are many charming streets and specialist shops selling cheese and other delicacies and family butchers have maintained a good business. Of course, commuters and those with a need to travel with easy motorway access are greatly attracted to such a beautiful old town. The town has become favoured as a location for TV and film crews, especially for the successful *Midsomer Murders* series.

Watlington Hill is managed by the National Trust and offers great walking in scrubland and wild chalk grassland. It is a centre for butterflies, in particular the silver spotted skipper, and well known for the free displays by the local red kites. Rather like the aerial equivalent of dolphins, they seem to take delight in occasional displays of mock combat to show off their flying skills to a delighted, uninvited audience. In spring crows constantly harass the kites to protect their territory and nesting sites, having more agility than the larger birds and making an impact – often literally!

North of Watlington is another spring-line village, Shirburn. This is distinguished by its fourteenth century castle, with full moat. Not open to the public, this is a rare example of a surviving medieval castle in the Chilterns. As with other places locally, such as Stonor, this was a centre for recusants in the sixteenth and seventeenth centuries during periods of suppression of the Catholic faith. During the eighteenth century the castle was in the forefront of the development of astronomy, with some of the earliest telescopes and an observatory. In recent times the castle has had a turbulent period, with disputes over ownership within the family of the Earl of Macclesfield, who no longer lives there. The Macclesfield family owned one of the finest medieval libraries in the world. This has been broken up and sold in recent years and included the rare Macclesfield Psalter which became a cause celebre to protect it from export, eventually being purchased by the Fitzwilliam Museum in Cambridge.

The next settlement is one of the highest in the area. Christmas Common is within the Watlington parish and is 790 feet above sea level. Its unusual name is thought to have derived from a Christmas Day truce during the Civil War – although this may not be correct as there was a family of this name locally. This is walking country, where red kites are probably more numerous than humans. Some locals have taken to feeding these beautiful birds, attracting them in large numbers – a practice not encouraged by the RSPB. The Oxfordshire Way passes through, and the Ridgeway and Icknield Way are both within a mile. This area is very popular at weekends with walkers and cyclists, when the local pub – The Fox and Hounds – is busy at lunch times.

Staying on high ground, following the ridge with magnificent views to the west, it is possible to park at Cowleaze Wood. From here there are numerous excellent footpaths. The

The Fox and Hounds Pub at Christmas Common.

Opposite: *Looking towards Shirburn from the top of the Chiltern scarp at Cowleaze Wood.*

views are huge, with another modern interloper – the omnipresent Didcot Power Station. Despite its impact, it does not detract too much from the wonderful vista across much of Oxfordshire.

This brings us to the most significant route of all – the development of the M40 through the Chilterns just beyond Aston Rowant. In the 1970s, a massive cutting, known as the "Stokenchurch Gap", or the "canyon", was carved through the chalk escarpment, enabling the fast link between London and Birmingham and then the North West. This was highly controversial, as it compromises some of the best landscape in southern Britain, the chosen route taking a direct line through the Aston Rowant Nature Reserve. At the time there was a massive campaign to promote a tunnel in preference to the cutting, but this was over-ruled by the Government. The decision was a wake up call to all conservationists and the M40 situation inspired much more high profile and influential campaigns with future projects. The irony is that this stretch of road was voted in 2010 as "one of the best views in the south" by BBC viewers, presumably unable to leave their cars for the real countryside. Also, despite the constant rumble of the traffic, the area is still a highly successful nature reserve and is regarded as one of the best locations to see red kites in the Chilterns. Sadly, it is not possible to walk

The impact of man – the M40 motorway and Didcot Power Station from Beacon Hill.

anywhere within about a mile of the motorway without being aware of the tremendous roar of the traffic. To get a real feel for the impact, take the old A40 up Aston Hill and then turn right just before Stokenchurch, to cross the motorway on a very high bridge with impressive, if shocking, views.

Close by is Beacon Hill, thrusting out into the plain with the motorway beneath. This is reputed to have been the scene of a major battle between the Saxons and Vikings but there is no real evidence. There is an old belief that juniper trees only flourish where a lot of blood has been spilt and there is an abundance of juniper across the entire hillside. It is a lovely landscape with good footpaths accessible from the car park at the Aston Rowant Nature Reserve, with excellent views and wonderful red kites.

Chinnor is a larger settlement with a population of nearly 6000, also owing its roots to the water springs at the base of the escarpment and its pre-historic position on the Icknield Way. Its later growth was based on cement production, which provided significant employment until 1989. There is still much evidence of cement quarries and pits at the base of Chinnor

Looking down on Chinnor from the top of Chinnor Hill.

Hill, now abandoned. This gives the village a much more industrial feel, when compared to other spring-line villages in the area – the echoes of a thriving, working town.

The village has a long history, with evidence back to Saxon times and a mention in the Domesday Book. The church dates back to the twelfth century, but is notable for its wonderful collection of brasses – some of which are relatively modern and even include memorials relating to the First World War. It is regarded as one of best collections of church brass in the UK.

Modern housing is now rising from the old workings, accommodating commuters that work in Oxford, Aylesbury, and London, as we are now within easy reach of the M40 motorway. As with so many other places along this route, driving road and rail links through the barrier of these hills has helped these towns economically by improving accessibility. It is well worth taking the road up Chinnor Hill and then to the nature reserve at the escarpment, which provides magnificent views across the entire vale, from Aylesbury and across Thame towards Oxford. Ancient barrows remind us of a distant past when the Ridgeway was the economic equivalent of our current motorways and rail routes. Chinnor also hosts the historic rail link with Princes Risborough, which has been preserved and runs during summer weekends.

Our exploration now moves further north, as the Chilterns scarp becomes more imposing. Below the scarp we find a string of small settlements that follow the spring-line. There is a pattern where the villages develop beside the source of fresh water, with cultivated land then lifting into the Chilterns, which are usually covered with dense beechwoods. The first of these is Bledlow, which reaches into its namesake Bledlow Ridge on the Chilterns plateau. These fall within the parish of Bledlow-cum-Saunderton. The spring, the Lyde Brook, was sufficient to power two mills in earlier times, one of which can still be visited. Holy Trinity church is most unusual, having two aisles, dating in parts back to 1200, with a particularly beautiful font. Obviously, carving shapes from the chalk hills must have been fashionable as we have another one here – a cross has been created at Wain Hill, high above the village.

Where a natural gap appears in the scarp, there has developed long term settlement. The town of Princes Risborough, which includes Monks Risborough, lies at the end of the link to West Wycombe and then High Wycombe, some eight miles to the south-east. Here the railway builders forged a way through, to link High Wycombe with Thame and Oxford, with the line opening in 1862. This enabled train links between London and Oxford for the first time, with passengers changing at Maidenhead. In 1906 a new direct line was opened through Gerrards Cross from Paddington. Today, the journey to London takes only 45 minutes with Chiltern Railways, making Princes Risborough another very popular country location for commuters.

An unusual feature of unknown origins is the Whiteleaf Cross, a chalk carving of a cross high above the town which was restored in 2003. This was recorded as early as 1700, but there

Opposite: *The vista from Chinnor Hill Nature Reserve.*

An ancient barrow above Princes Risborough at the crest of the scarp.

Below: *At the top of the Whiteleaf Hill cross feature above Princes Risborough.*

is little evidence of its past or reasons for its presence. One theory is that it was cut from a natural chalk slope by soldiers passing time during the Civil War. The feature is actually on Whiteleaf Hill, just outside the town, very close to an ancient tumulus burial, suggesting that there might be an earlier link as with those elsewhere on chalkland sites across southern England.

The origins of the name Risborough relate to "brushwood covered hills" – the addition of Princes derived from the period when the manor was taken by the Black Prince, the son of Edward III. In 1086, the Domesday Book there are recorded a collection of small settlements including two watermills, probably with a population of around 200 in total. The community was based around a Royal Manor, held by successive kings and princes from Norman times and probably used primarily as a base for hunting. It was only after the fall of Charles I that this manor was eventually sold to the City of London as part of the reparation terms after the Civil War, ending a continuous period of 600 years as a royal estate.

The church dates back to the thirteenth century and like many in the area, was built on the foundations of an earlier church. It was common for the Normans to destroy much of any pre-existing Saxon churches and re-build on the same site to ensure some continuity as a place

The woods in winter above Princes Risborough.

of worship. Built of flint and stone with Tudor additions, a key feature is the original thirteenth century windows – the spire is modern as the previous one fell down in the nineteenth century. Also well worth a visit are the wood carvings of the stations of the cross in the distinctive St Teresa's Catholic church which are particularly mentioned by Pevsner, even though these are relatively modern. The National Trust now owns the Manor House, a classic example of a seventeenth century red brick house of elegant proportions.

Just to the south, at Lacey Green, lies the oldest working smock windmill left in the entire country, sited high on the Chilterns ridge. Derelict by 1970, the windmill was rescued by a dedicated team of volunteers and restored over many years, retaining much of the original features and machinery, some of which dates back to 1650. The mill is only open to visitors on Sundays and Bank Holidays but is well worth the diversion. There are a few other windmills surviving in the Chilterns: as well as the site at Pitstone near Ivinghoe, another is under restoration at Great Haseley towards Thame, close to the M40.

Between Princes Risborough and Wendover lies the village of Ellesborough, nestling under the scarp of some wonderful rolling chalk hills. Very striking is another Beacon Hill – obviously named for its appropriateness for this purpose in earlier days, being visible to the

Looking down the steep sides of Beacon Hill towards the site of Cymbeline's Castle.

north and south for many miles. Beside this is an old motte and bailey castle, strangely referred to as Cymbeline's Castle. There is no obvious connection to the Shakespeare play, but there was a first century king across southern England known as Kymbelinus and the nearby hamlets are known as Great and Little Kimble.

The hills around this area are full of the marks of previous occupation, with dykes and terraces and another iron age fort at Pulpit Hill. Nearby is the Grangelands Nature Reserve where the grasslands are particularly rich in invertebrates, including the marbled white and chalk hill blue butterflies and populations of glow worms. The large Roman edible snail can also be found in the grassland and would no doubt be very attractive to any French visitors.

Wandering these hills on a misty winter morning, one can feel that there has been a human presence here for a very long time and this might have been a significant boundary or trading route. One can really feel a sense of history, of being somewhere that has been touched by humans for many thousands of years.

Above: *The chalk is at the surface across Beacon Hill.*

Above left: *Ellesborough church below Beacon Hill.*

The ancient Ridgeway creates a mysterious atmosphere.

Opposite: *The view of Coombe Hill and its monument from Beacon Hill.*

While in the area, divert to the Chiltern Brewery at Terrick, just north of Ellesborough, to sample some beer brewed using traditional methods. Founded in 1980, this was one of the pioneers of small scale independent brewing that has now becoming so popular.

Approaching Wendover is Coombe Hill, a significant landmark on the scarp as it has a large monument, erected in 1904 as a memorial to local men who died in the Boer War. The monument is an iconic Buckinghamshire landmark, at 260m above sea level. It sits at one of the highest and most striking spurs of the Chilterns, commanding a wide view of the Vale of Aylesbury. On a clear day it can be seen from the Berkshire Downs and Salisbury Plain to the south-west, the Cotswolds to the west and, on very clear days, the Malvern Hills. The view overlooks Chequers to the south, the country home of the Prime Minister, and extends as far round to the east as Ivinghoe and as far to the north as the eye can reach. Being in such a prominent position, it has twice been badly damaged by lightning strikes, until proper conductors were fitted. It is also the scene for an annual event – The Coombe Hill Run – which takes place on the first Sunday of June every year. Starting and finishing in Wendover, the runners have to scale Coombe Hill and back. The site is also home to the first ever geocache in England. There are good footpaths and a car park close to the summit, which is worthy of a visit just for the magnificent views.

Looking across the vale from Coombe Hill.

The monument was built to commemorate the Boer War.

Coombe Hill was gifted to the National Trust, having been part of the Chequers estate. As one would expect, there is a lot of evidence of security throughout the area, but the estate can be seen from some of the surrounding hills and some footpaths run quite close by, including the Ridgeway. During the Second World War, the house was deemed to be too dangerous for Churchill as it was exposed to air attack, although this never happened. There are many links to Cromwell. The estate was gifted by the Lee family to the nation in 1917 during the era of David Lloyd George to become the country home to the incumbent Prime Minister and to host visiting heads of state and other international figures. The parkland setting around the house is exquisite, nestling between Coombe Hill and Beacon Hill.

The town of Wendover probably has a history back into distant times, being a classic example of a spring-line settlement. Indeed, the origins of the name relate to "white water", referring to the stream emerging from the chalk hillside. Two watermills were recorded in the Domesday Book, probably as fulling mills to stretch and felt newly woven cloth. Many of the houses are of medieval origin, notably the thatched Anne Boleyn Cottages on the Tring road. There are many Victorian additions such as the distinctive clock tower at the end of the High

Market day in Wendover.

Graceful houses line the streets in Wendover.

Street, now the tourist office. The town hosts regular markets that provide a colourful backdrop to the wide street, although this now feels much more like a village, with a modest population of around 7000.

As with Tring to the north, Wendover sits in one of the few natural gaps in the scarp, causing it to be a natural hub for transport routes. The main line to Aylesbury from London runs through the town, making it highly desirable as a location for commuting. However, this has now resulted in great controversy as the route has been designated for the newly proposed HS2 high speed link, so that the new line literally runs almost through the town. At the time of writing there are major local campaigns to prevent the route from becoming a reality. The route following the Misbourne Valley would pass through some beautiful landscape and would have an enormous impact on the Chilterns.

The walking is excellent, with over 33 miles of footpaths within the parish boundary. The walk through the bluebell woods to Dunsmore is particularly popular in the spring and autumn. The five mile length of the Wendover Arm of the Grand Union Canal is under restoration and provides an excellent walking route for those not wishing to tackle any hills. With much wildlife, this is a most pleasant walk at any time of the year.

Bluebells cover much of the Chilterns in early May.

The hamlets and woods near Wendover are beautiful even in winter.

Following the broad line of the Ridgeway, we now leave Wendover. This is the closest section to Aylesbury, which is very evident in the valley below the ridge. Wendover Woods provide a wonderful amenity, managed by the Forestry Commission. There are miles of cycling and waymarked routes with a small café and play areas for children. This is the highest part of the Chilterns – at Haddington Hill being 267 metres high. The woods offer mixed varieties and there are regular events such a fungus forays and guided walks. At the southern end is Boddington Hill, directly above Wendover, with a significant Iron Age fort. The immediate surroundings of these woods are a wonderful example of the very best Chiltern landscape, with quiet lanes descending through beech woods through small hamlets such as The Hale and Kingsash.

A major local employer is RAF Halton, which is today a major centre for training RAF personnel. Halton House, once one of the many mansions set up by the Rosthchilds, is now the Officers Mess and was originally used for training officers in Kitchener's Army in the First World War. The site of this complex rests quite high on the scarp below the Wendover Woods, so the views across the Vale of Aylesbury are impressive.

At Tring is the Bulbourne valley – and one of the few Chiltern rivers. This provided one of the few natural routes through the Chilterns between London and the Midlands. It is not surprising that this valley was selected for one of the pioneering canal building schemes. It

was the Grand Junction Canal which really provided the transport infrastructure to bring goods from the industrial conurbations of the North and Midlands to the capital. The Act of Parliament to authorise its construction was passed in 1793 and work started in the same year. The canal follows the course of the river through Bourne End and Berkhamsted. At Cow Roast Lock, near Aldbury, the canal reaches the three-mile long summit level, having risen through 54 locks since Brentford. Now known as the Grand Union Canal, this is today a popular route for pleasure boating with very little commercial traffic, busy in summer with colourful narrowboats.

As well as being attractive to canal builders, the natural gap in the hills also determined the route for the early railways. The main lines from Birmingham to London run through the valley, with a convenient station at Tring now providing a fast route for commuters into London. The numbers of parked cars at the station are testament to the extent that commuters

A typical Chiltern landscape near Wendover.

A barge on the Grand Union Canal at Tring.

The canal wharf at New Mill in Tring.

At the canal junction with the old link to Wendover.

The church of St Peter and Paul at Tring.

live in this area. Of course, the roads pre-existed and developed into the main A41 today.

Tring lies where the ancient Icknield Way crosses the Roman Akeman Street. The Manor of Tring is described in the Domesday survey of 1086, but it is thought that this was an important centre in Saxon times. In 1682 the mansion designed by Christopher Wren was built and one resident was Lawrence Washington, great-great-grandfather of George Washington, the first President of the USA. In the late nineteenth century the estate became the home of the Rothschild family, whose mark on this area is very evident.

The Grand Junction Canal wharf opened at New Mill in 1796. Trade developed quickly and in 1823 the Silk Mill in Brook Street was constructed by William Kay. The four Tring reservoirs – Wilstone, Tringford, Startops End and Marsworth – were built to supply water for the canal. These have been a National Nature Reserve since 1955 and now have become wildlife attractions, especially for waterfowl and migrating species, with excellent access and footpaths.

The town developed further with the construction of the railway in 1835 by the London and Birmingham Company. The engineer, George Stephenson, completed the digging of the Tring cutting and on completion of the railway, Tring lay just one hour away from London.

In 1872, the Rosthchilds moved to Tring Park. As enlightened local landowners, they built new houses and provided a clean water supply, having an architectural impact on the town with its English-style lodges and houses. This also started a long association with natural history as Lionel Walter Rosthchild set up one of the earliest collections of specimens, with a museum opening to the public in 1892. Rothschild used to ride around Tring in a zebra-drawn carriage. In 1937 before his death, Walter donated the museum to the nation. Today, this explains why the Natural History Museum operates with its own provincial museum in Tring. This is well worth a visit to see the amazing range of specimens collected from the Victorian era as well as having a modern dimension with new displays. The mansion was later sold and became the Tring School for the Performing Arts and the park of 300 acres is now cared for by the Woodland Trust, providing valuable open space.

In addition to Tring, during the second half of the nineteenth century the Rothschilds acquired and constructed a further six grand houses in the Vale of Aylesbury. Of these, the house at Aston Clinton is no longer standing, Mentmore Towers and Eyethrope Pavilion are in private hands, Waddesdon Manor and Ascott House are held by the National Trust and Halton House is an RAF Officers' Mess.

Modern Tring (population 13,000) is largely residential, but its industries include milling, egg-packing and electronics. Heygate's Tring mill processes 100,000 tons of wheat per annum and has 80 employees. The town is also attractive to a large commuter population, given direct access to London by train and being so close to the Chilterns with its country houses. The regular antiques auctions also attract many visitors to the town centre and Tring is known to be one of the leading auction centres in the Home Counties. Recently a new local history museum has opened in the Market Place which has very good displays and references to the development of Tring and the surrounding areas.

Close to the north, and directly underneath the Bridgewater Monument on the scarp, lies Aldbury. This is a classic English village, with its two pubs, large village pond and even a pair of stocks. The seventeenth-century cottages that comprise the Valiant Trooper pub have served as alehouses for several centuries. The first traceable evidence dates back to 1752 when the pub – then known as the Royal Oak – was left in the will of one John Barnes. Its next owner was

The landscape at Tring Park.

Isaac Dell Master, whose initials "ID" and the date "1769" can be seen carved in the brickwork alongside the main front window. The name changed to The Trooper Alehouse in 1803 – rumoured to be because the Duke of Wellington met his troops here to discuss tactics. It became The Valiant Trooper in 1878.

To the north of Aldbury, the shape of the hills forms a natural amphitheatre that embraces some magnificent countryside with rolling fields and traditional farms, all overlooked by the beech wooded ridge. At Aldbury Nowers is a nature reserve and the chalk hillsides throughout this charming corner also provide rare species of wild plants. A diversion along the Ridgeway Path is recommended to get the real "feel" for this landscape, with good views towards Ivinghoe Beacon. At Incombe Hole, on the flanks of the main ridge is a wonderful example of a dramatic dry valley, with exceptionally steep sides formed through the freezing and thawing of water during the Ice Age.

Today, Aldbury is a popular place for filming, being used for *Bridget Jones Diary* and episodes of *Inspector Morse* and *Midsomer Murders*. The main house in the village, Stock House, has an element of notoriety, once being the home of Victor Lownes of *Playboy* fame.

Local villages developed along the spring line. Directly below the beacon is Ivinghoe, a charming old village with some fine medieval houses and an excellent church with an unusual spire. Very nearby is the Pitstone Windmill, owned by the National Trust and occasionally open to visitors at weekends. This is a good example of a post mill, where the frame of the entire mill was rotated around a central hub, aided by a long shaft with a wheel attachment to aid movement. Thought to date back to 1627, it is believed to be one of the oldest surviving windmills in the country. It was badly damaged by a storm in 1902 and became

Opposite: *Aldbury.*

Aldbury church with the Chilterns scarp in the background.

Incombe Hole is a very deep and sudden valley caused originally by melting ice.

Ivinghoe village and church from the Ridgeway Path.

Pitstone Windmill.

The Bridgewater Monument overlooks the scarp and offers magnificent views from the top.

derelict, until it was purchased in 1937 by the National Trust and then carefully restored by volunteers.

Most of this area is part of the Ashridge Estate, managed by the National Trust. There are very extensive beechwoods with good access facilities and an Information Centre near the Bridgewater Monument. The monument was built in 1832 to commemorate the third Duke of Bridgewater, a pioneer of eighteenth-century canal-building. This is open to the public and the climb up is worth the effort as the views along the scarp are very good. Many of the walks are waymarked and include routes for wheelchair users. A visit in May will not disappoint as the bluebells here are exceptional, as are the beech trees in the autumn. With the support of the National Trust, local grazing using traditional Galloway cattle has been re-introduced onto the surrounding grasslands, bringing back a lost tradition and with great biodiversity benefits.

Our Ridgeway exploration concludes in Hertfordshire, at the terminal point of the Ridgeway Path at Ivinghoe Beacon, 757 feet above sea level, just to the north of Tring. This prominent hill is not unlike standing on a great coastal headland, reaching out from the main range as a peninsula into the surrounding plains. It is a good vantage point to imagine a great lake formed from meltwater during the Ice Age. To the north are the largely flat lands of Hertfordshire and Bedfordshire; looking east one notices the chalk shape of a lion etched into the scarp, heralding the nearby Whipsnade estate with its zoo. To the west is the Vale of Aylesbury, with the town very evident just a few miles distant, with the beautiful village of Ivinghoe close by with its church tower very distinct, with Mentmore a few miles beyond. The southern aspect completes the picture, with extensive views following the scarp of the hills visible for many miles. It is highly recommended that a visit is made to this spot – it is easily accessible by car with a road climbing from Ivinghoe onto the Ridgeway with parking being fairly convenient. It is worth the one mile walk along the Ridgeway to reach the beacon itself as this is a great introduction to the area. It still has a sense of being very ancient, remaining open ground, with the cattle drovers road intact. It is not hard to imagine the traders, soldiers and pilgrims that have passed this way over 300 generations.

This route, scarcely more than fifty miles, is better described by Rupert Brooke in his poem. "The Chilterns":

Sheep graze above Ivinghoe Church on Ivinghoe Beacon.

The beacon marks the terminus of the Ridgeway Long Distance Path.

Ivinghoe Beacon stands like a headland into the surrounding plains.

65

Descending down the scarp towards Britwell Salome near Watlington.

THE CHILTERNS

Your hands, my dear, adorable,
Your lips of tenderness
-Oh, I've loved you faithfully and well,
Three years, or a bit less.
It wasn't a success.

Thank God, that's done! and I'll take the road,
Quit of my youth and you,
The Roman road to Wendover
By Tring and Lilley Hoo,
As a free man may do.

For youth goes over, the joys that fly,
The tears that follow fast;
And the dirtiest things we do must lie
Forgotten at the last;
Even love goes past.

What's left behind I shall not find,
The splendor and the pain;
The splash of sun, the shouting wind,
And the brave sting of rain,
I may not meet again.

Woods at Stonor.

Typical woodland scene near Christmas Common.

But the years, that take the best away,
Give something in the end;
And a better friend than love have they,
For none to mar or mend,
That have themselves to friend.

I shall desire and I shall find
The best of my desires;
The autumn road, the mellow wind
That soothes the darkening shires,
And laughter, and inn-fires.

White mist about the black hedgerows,
The slumbering Midland plain,
The silence where the clover grows,
And the dead leaves in the lane,
Certainly, these remain.

And I shall find some girl perhaps,
And a better one than you,
With eyes as wise, but kindlier,
With lips as soft, but true.
And I daresay she will do.

Rupert Brooke

67

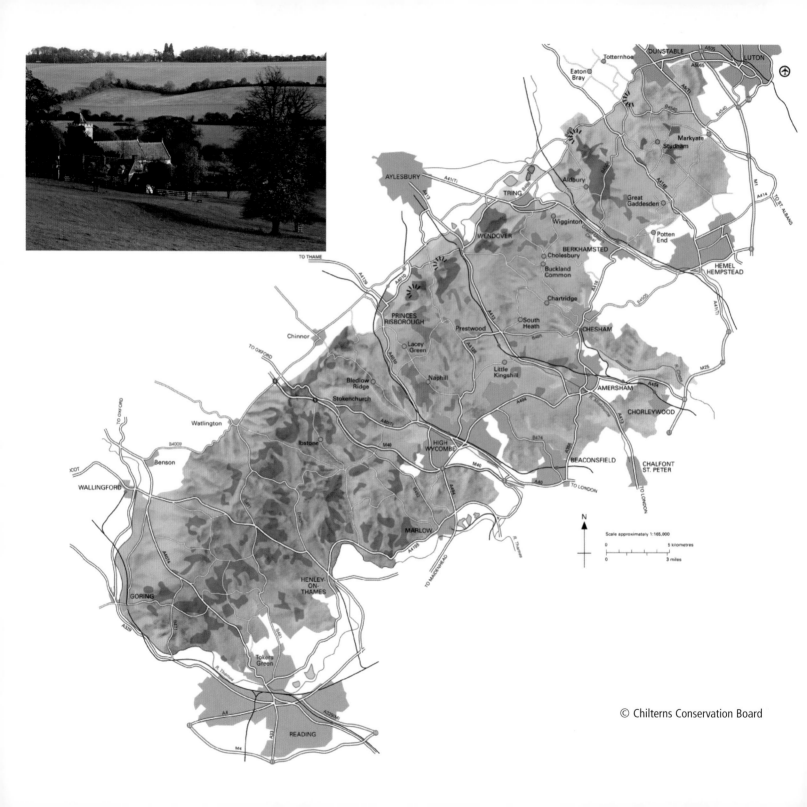

TO THAME

TO OXFORD

TO OXFORD

ASCOT

N

Scale approximately 1:165,000

0   5 kilometres

0   3 miles

© Chilterns Conservation Board

DUNSTABLE
LUTON
Totternhoe
Eaton Bray
Markyate
Studham
AYLESBURY
TRING
Aldbury
Great Gaddesden
Wigginton
WENDOVER
Potten End
BERKHAMSTED
Cholesbury
Buckland Common
HEMEL HEMPSTEAD
Chartridge
TO ST ALBANS
PRINCES RISBOROUGH
Prestwood
South Heath
CHESHAM
Chinnor
Lacey Green
Little Kingshill
Bledlow Ridge
Naphill
Stokenchurch
AMERSHAM
CHORLEYWOOD
Watlington
Ibstone
HIGH WYCOMBE
Benson
BEACONSFIELD
CHALFONT ST. PETER
WALLINGFORD
TO LONDON
TO LONDON
MARLOW
TO MAIDENHEAD
GORING
HENLEY-ON-THAMES
R. Thames
Tokers Green
READING

The Bridgewater Monument from Ashridge House.

Opposite: The church at Hughenden Manor where Disraeli is buried.

CHAPTER THREE
THE CENTRAL CHILTERNS

Having travelled up and over the scarp of the Chilterns, we continue to explore the Ashridge Estate. Leaving the Vales of Oxford and Aylesbury behind us, we come into a typical landscape of high chalk plateau interspersed with deep, but usually dry, valleys. With the advent of the railways following the valley floor, small villages developed rapidly into large settlements such as Amersham, Chesham and Berkhamsted, with High Wycombe as the most prominent town in the entire Chilterns.

The Quaker Meeting House at Jordans.

Beech woods at Ashridge.

Traditional small furniture factory at the Chiltern Open Air Museum.

There is a strong tradition of religious non-conformity in this area, with a major influence over the early development of new Protestant groups, providing some of the earliest settlers to the New World from places like Penn and the birthplace of the Quakers at Jordans.

This area is also heavily wooded, with beech woods being the predominant example, having once had an important economic purpose in providing ideal timber for making furniture in the factories at High Wycombe. These woods are man-made, as the natural native woodland was mixed and then replaced for commercial purposes. Local craftsmen, known as "bodgers", would turn green timber on a pole lathe into finished shapes for the chair making factories. These were known as "billets", which is the derivation of the often used "crooked billet" as the name for local pubs in the Chilterns. The legs, stretchers, spindles and arm supports were fashioned from beech wood using pole lathes set up in the woods. These components were then transported to the factories for final assembly. There were also local styles, so that a Chilterns chair would be very different in style from a chair made in another region. Even within the Chilterns there were favoured styles, with Chesham chairs sometimes being different from those from High Wycombe.

The bodgers worked outside in the woods, close to the site of the timber being worked. They would bid at auctions to purchase a stand of timber and then work it out, clearing the area for new planting. They would set up small shelters to provide protection from the weather, but usually returned home every night, taking a load of the finished article back for collection and onward transport to High Wycombe. The very last bodgers survived until the 1950s.

Although the Chiltern area is primarily chalk, in many places a layer of clay, known as Reading Clay, overlies the chalk and this sustained brick making, especially in Victorian times

during the boom in demand for new housing in London. This was a hard life, usually using child labour in Victorian times. The clay had to be dug in winter when it was workable, and then laid into moulds and turned into the hot kilns to dry them. There are still a few traditional hand-made brick companies in the Chesham area, servicing demand for restoration work. However, most of these industries have vanished, with large scale arable agriculture and occasional sheep rearing being the primary activity alongside the extensive service industries to support such an affluent population.

Traditional hand-made bricks from a nineteenth century school.

Starting from the area lying to the north of the A41 near Tring, this chapter takes in the localities of Berkhamsted and the large parklands of Ashridge, down through Chesham, Amersham and the Chalfonts, to the Missendens, Beaconsfield and High Wycombe. Given its proximity to London and, in particular, the M25 and M40 motorways, there is a distinctive metropolitan influence. The towns are close enough to offer commuters easy access and the more prestigious properties in the secluded valleys are clearly based on the wealth of London. For example, some houses have facilities to land privately owned helicopters.

This does not compromise the beauty of the area, although it does mean that this corner of the Chilterns can be quite busy at weekends as the journey from London and its western suburbs can be less than an hour. A good example of an unspoilt landscsape is the wonderful Ashridge Estate to the north of Berkhamsted. Now managed by the National Trust, the estate is massive, and covers 20 square kilometres from Ivinghoe in the north and centred on the Ashridge Business School that was once an ancient priory and, in later times, the country home of the Egerton family. The estate offers extensive areas of beech woods and parkland, with abundant wild deer that seem to be conditioned to human company. In May, this area is one the finest for bluebells and in the autumn the colours can be spectacular. The entire area

Parkland within the Ashridge Estate.

Fungi at Ashridge.

offers endless walking options with a good visitor centre near the Bridgewater Monument, featured in the previous chapter. There is a lot of interest as the landscape changes from woodland into open spaces with rolling valleys, especially at the Golden Valley near Little Gaddesden. The National Trust are very active and there are usually many events of interest, with an annual countryside fair every September with demonstrations of ancient Chiltern crafts and farming techniques.

This is also the location of the Ashridge Golf Club that was once the base for the famous golfer Henry Cotton. This area is well worth a visit and has proved to be a very popular location for many films and TV dramas, being close to the studios in London.

The local centre is Berkhamsted, in the Bulbourne Valley. This town has historical significance as the main base for William the Conqueror prior to his coronation at Westminster Abbey in December 1066. Following his crossing of the Thames at Wallingford, he accepted the final surrender of the Saxons at Berkhamsted, to then take London from the north. As a result, the Norman influence was rooted here from an early stage with land being requisitioned for new manorial estates. Berkhamsted became a great favourite country retreat for the royal dynasties until the Plantagenets. The castle was started in 1066 and is now in ruins, but in its heyday it was the equivalent of today's Windsor as their country base. The Black Prince, Henry III and Richard III all spent time here, before it was abandoned in the late fifteenth century. As with Wallingford, its castle is just a ruin today but the extent of its scale in its prime is easy to imagine. In St Peter's church is a tomb which is believed to be that

The 18th hole at the Ashridge Golf Course, one of the top courses in the UK.

On the golf course in Golden Valley.

The ruined castle at Berkhamsted, base for William the Conqueror.

Below: *The tomb in St Peter's Church.*

of Henry of Berkhamsted who was one of the Black Prince's lieutenants at the Battle of Crecy – there is some irony as Charles de Gaulle lived at Berkhamsted while exiled from France in 1941-2. This church also hosts a very poignant memorial to three young brothers, all killed in action within months in the First World War; the sheer scale of losses, recorded on another memorial, is staggering for such a small town.

Nearby is Castle Wharf, where the Grand Union Canal passes through in parallel with the High Street and the railway lines from London, reinforcing the concentration of major communication links through the few gaps available through the Chilterns. Beside the canal, near the Crystal Palace public house, is one of the few genuine totem poles in England, commissioned by the Alsford family in 1968. The town itself has many ancient properties, including what is thought to be the oldest shop in England, dated at around 1290, and the sixteenth-century Pennyfarthing Hotel. The author Graham Greene was raised here, being at Berkhamsted School where his father was the Headmaster. Another notable building is the Art Deco Rex Cinema, a 1930s' picture house that has been fully restored with its original features.

Lying high on a ridge to the south-west, towards Wendover, is the village of Cholesbury. This ridge also links several other villages along a linear alignment – Hawridge, Buckland Common and St Leonards. This elevated position also sustained a windmill, now a dwelling.

This was once a favourite location for the Bloomsbury Group and several well known artists and thinkers stayed here – among them D.H Lawrence and Bertrand Russell.

Cholesbury is also the site of one of the largest Iron Age forts in the Chilterns, with impressive enclosure walls very much in evidence. There are mixed accounts of its origins, but it is accepted that the fort was probably of very early date as Palaeolithic artefacts have been found. Being such a strong defensive site, it is likely that this was of importance until the Roman invasion, with some evidence of medieval occupation, and St Lawrence's church lies within its boundary.

The extensive Cholesbury Common is also enclosed by extensive beech woods that once supplied the furniture factories at High Wycombe. What was once a typical rural village, with water from wells, orchards, small farms and thriving brickworks has given way to very expensive homes with easy access to the capital and motorways.

It is apparent in this part of the Chilterns that the pattern of early settlement favoured the ridges rather than the valleys, where larger towns such as Berkhamsted and Chesham have developed in more recent times. Lying to the south of Cholesbury is another area of linear

The unusual totem pole stands beside the canal at Berkhamsted.

The Grand Union Canal at Berkhamsted.

Far left: *The windmill used by the Bloomsbury Group at Cholesbury.*

Left: *Deep ditches still encircle the Iron Age fort at Cholesbury Ring.*

The cottages beside the common at the hamlet of The Lee, home to the Liberty family.

Below: *The people of Fromelles still remember the sacrifice made by the young men of The Lee in the First World War.*

hamlets, defined by geography at higher elevation north-west of Chesham. Chartridge is only about two miles away – along the ancient route between Chesham and Wendover with scattered farms which are now mostly expensive homes. In the seventeenth century local maps suggest that there were at least 17 working farms. By the nineteenth century cottage industries were emerging, notably lace making. In the later nineteenth and early twentieth centuries many village people, who would in earlier times have worked on the land, moved to industries centred on nearby Chesham, for example, boot and shoe manufacture and brush making.

Further west is The Lee, with Lee Common and Lee Gate. These picturesque small hamlets mask their tragic history. The Liberty family, famous for the London store, have lived at the manor since the early 1900s. As with so many villages across the country, all the young men working on the estate signed up for service in the First World War and were mobilised within the same regiment, the 2nd Bucks Battallion. During the Battle of Fromelles in July 1916, together with the Somme, just a few weeks later, in total 30 men from The Lee were wiped out. This was an enormous blow to such a small community.

Having crossed southwards from the Bulbourne Valley, lying just south is another of the few river valleys that have driven so much human activity – the Chess Valley and another town, Chesham, close by its neighbour, Amersham. It lies at the confluence of three, quite deep dry valleys that were once overflows for glacial meltwaters. The Chess River emerges here as a stream, now flowing in culverts under the town, before emerging towards Latimer in its natural state, as wonderful water meadows for some miles, offering a good wetland habitat and even watercress beds. The Chess Valley Walk is a splendid way to experience this lovely valley. Contrary to expectations, the derivation of the name Chesham is not from this stream – rather the stream was named after the Saxon name for the town. In Victorian times this stream powered several mills, especially producing paper for the market in London.

Chesham has a long history, with much pre-historic evidence and Iron Age activity. The Normans were very active, probably influenced by the nearby importance of Berkhamsted Castle. The oldest medieval part of the town is known as the Nap, in the area of twelfth century St Mary's church today. There is evidence of many pudding stones in the area of this knoll as well as Neolithic and Saxon remains, so this natural feature may well have had a long religious significance. Religious dissent also runs deep as in the sixteenth century, Thomas Harding was burnt at the stake for heresy. This seems to have led to a tradition of non-conformity, with many leaving to join the English colonies in America in 1643. Among these early émigrés was Aquila Chase, whose descendents created the Chase Manhattan Bank. This

The small Chess stream runs through the town of Chesham.

tradition was maintained into the eighteenth and nineteenth century with Chesham becoming a major centre for the emergence of the Baptists, Methodists and Quakers. The local Chesham Museum is worth a visit to see the history of the town and how the area has influenced social and religious reform.

The town is affectionately known for its four "B's" – boots, brushes, beer and Baptists. This may have once been the case, but not so today. Chesham is no longer dependent on cottage industries, which have been long lost. With the opening of the Metropolitan line to Amersham, access to London has become very easy and the clean air and calm of the Chilterns are a tempting haven for a country home. The town has all the high quality amenities to service a wealthy population with pedestrian access to stores and an abundance of leisure facilities, including the Elgiva Theatre, all within easy reach. It is close enough to London to be designated as Green Belt and as such

The medieval tomb in the church at Chesham.

Left: *The old part of Chesham is known as the Nap.*

future growth beyond the current population of 20,000 is strictly controlled – making it even more desirable. The town also services all the surrounding villages – also favourite places for commuters – such as Latimer and Chenies.

The Chess Valley continues as an idyllic contrast to the surrounding hills, its peace shattered once it meets the M25 to enter the Colne Valley. Here there are leafy hamlets, notably Latimer, Chenies and Sarratt. Discreet small estates, once farms, provide handy country escapes within easy reach of the capital. Latimer has some history, as Charles I was taken to Latimer House shortly after his capture, on his way to his trial in London. The village is quite attractive with its small green and water pump. Chenies is famous for its Manor, originally home to the Cheyne family and recommended warmly by Pevsner. Open to the public, it has been used for many films and TV series and boasts a maze within its beautiful gardens. Chenies village was originally an estate village looking across the Chess Valley. The church has some fine monuments and tombs to the Russell family.

In this area, many large properties are tucked away. When George Smiley, in *Tinker, Tailor, Soldier, Spy* by John le Carre refers to Sarratt as the location for the "safe" house to de-brief spies, one can imagine just such places and wonder if they really do exist, just an hour from London and close to Northolt airfield. The church was used as one of the wedding venues in *Four Weddings and a Funeral*.

Lying just south of Chesham – so close that they are almost one complex – lies Amersham, with the Misbourne Valley running down to the Chalfonts. The town splits into two very distinctive parts: Old Amersham, as the name suggests, was the original settlement beside the

The attractive green at Latimer with its Victorian well.

Right: *Ancient alleyways lead off the main street in Old Amersham.*

Opposite: *Typical Chiltern scenery in the Misbourne Valley.*

River Misbourne. This would, at one time, have been totally separated from Chesham until the hill between was developed as a result of the railways – so Amersham-on-the-Hill is a Victorian invention, since developed into its own substantial town with a population of nearly 18000 in total. The Old Town has a fine Town Hall astride the main street, with many old buildings. Originally Saxon it has a similar history as other Chiltern towns – Norman conquest, Civil War conflict and religious dissent. In the sixteenth century the "Lollards" were rounded up and burnt at the stake for their Protestant beliefs, probably spawning a resentment that carried through the later generations and fuelled the strong non-conformist sentiment.

The railways created wealth and towns developed from a rural community, with Amersham being the further-

The Misbourne Valley at Little Missenden.

Right: *Local opposition to the HS2 project at Little Missenden.*

most reach for the London Underground, with Chiltern Railways also providing a faster service. Throughout this part of the Chilterns, the busy time of day will be early morning when commuters vie for space in the massive car parks, followed by the slightly later "school run". The entire way of life is a consequence of railways and motorways, making the area wealthy and desirable. It is therefore no surprise that the proposed HS2 railway link that will follow the Misbourne Valley is fiercely resisted, just as the original railway was subject to widespread indignation in its time. If this does go ahead, it will have a devastating impact on the landscape and biodiversity in a designated AONB, which is setting an unfortunate precedent for the future.

Rather like the Chalfonts, the collective name of "the Missendens" is used to describe very tiny Little Missenden and its much larger neighbour, Great Missenden. These lie to the west of Amersham, higher up the Misbourne Valley. The valley is typical of a Chiltern landscape, with large areas of beech woodland and gentle pastures enclosing a charming settlement of fine houses; no wonder there is so much local opposition to the prospect of high speed trains.

The name Missenden derives from the "valley where the marsh plants grow" indicating an earlier period when the valley would have been quite wet. Little Missenden is an ancient settlement and the church's strong Saxon features survived the Norman transformation so common in many churches. This church is unusual in having wall paintings that have survived from the twelfth century. It is thought that in the early Norman period the clergy were imported from France and the services were in Latin, so the native population, obligated as serfs to attend the church by their Norman landlords, had no understanding of the services – hence the wall paintings to depict Biblical scenes. There are several hamlets in the locality, some with marvellous names such as Mop End and Hotley Bottom. This is another highly desirable location to live and has attracted local artists and musicians to create a local Arts Festival which draws support from a wide area. The Little Missenden Arts Festival started in 1959 and has built a very high reputation attracting well known performers from the world of classical music with most performances in the church, beside the Misbourne river.

Great Missenden is perhaps more famous in recent times through its association with the famous author Roald Dahl, who lived here for most of his adult life. Gipsy House and is where most of his stories were crafted, in a small shed at the bottom of his garden. He had a strict regime of working for two hours every day, seated in an adapted armchair. Having been injured in the Second World War when his Hurricane fighter crashed, he was one of the first people to have an artificial hip. The popular Roald Dahl Museum and Story Centre, in the

The beautiful Misbourne Valley in winter.

The Roald Dahl Museum in Great Missenden, where the great writer lived.

The museum has captured the spirit of Dahl very well.
Below: *The chair used by Roald Dahl is now a great attraction.*

FLUSHBUNKINGLY GLORIUMPTIOUS

Café Twit

High Street, is a brilliant testimony to his slightly anarchic writing. Only open since 2005, it was awarded as the "Best Small Visitor Attraction" in 2008. The building has a full size giant – the famous BFG – painted onto its façade, depicting the scale of his exploits in blowing dreams into people's bedrooms at night! Walking tours from the museum take in various local landmarks including Dahl's grave at the local church. The family tradition has been maintained as his grand-daughter, Sophie Dahl, lives locally. A visit to this museum is recommended, especially for children of all ages.

Great Missenden owes much to its position on the main communication routes from London to Aylesbury and more recently the railways, with its own station on the Chiltern Railways. This makes it yet another very attractive commuter belt location, although these are distinctly posh commuters given the local price of property. Originally a religious centre with its own abbey, this was destroyed during the Dissolution of the Monasteries and was rebuilt as a Georgian mansion which is now part of the University of Buckingham.

The Misbourne Valley is far too grand for such a small stream that is prone to drying up on occasions. It was obviously once a serious river, probably fed by melting ice sheets lying to the north in the last Ice Age. After Amersham, it flows down to an area collectively known as "The Chalfonts" – although Little Chalfont is more about Amersham and a product of the

Victorian growth of the railways. Chalfont St Giles retains a genteel feel with its village pond and greenery alongside the small shops that have survived, proud of its good record in the "Best Kept Village" competitions. It was here that Milton fled when the plague ravaged London, to write *Paradise Lost*. His cottage is now a museum. Although the Chilterns still influence the landscape with rolling hills and chalk streams, the towns and villages now have a distinct metropolitan feel – typical of the Home Counties with mid-twentieth century red-brick houses behind well-kept hedges.

Nearby the interesting Chiltern Open Air Museum has been developed in the grounds of the University of Buckingham on a 45 acre site. Mostly run by volunteers, the exhibits go back as far as 2000 years, with a convincing replica of an Iron Age Roundhouse. This exhibit helps us imagine just how the various defensive sites across the Chilterns may have looked when occupied. Most of the buildings are in fact original and have been re-built within the site. The layout is helpful and includes woodland walks and open spaces. It is interesting to visit an original Toll House from 1826, taken from the main Oxford to London road at High Wycombe. In addition to a complete farm, there are excellent exhibits about the furniture industry with a typical small factory for chair making. This demonstrates how the components were assembled and the tools used, with good exhibits about the life of the "bodgers."

Milton's House at Chalfont St Giles, where Paradise Lost *was written.*

Left: *The village green and shops at Chalfont St Giles.*

Ancient cottage and chapel reconstructed at the Chiltern Open Air Museum.

The graves of William Penn and other early Quakers occupy a peaceful setting in beech woods at Jordans.

Chalfont St Peter is a more substantial town, lying in an elbow of land between two major motorways, the M25 and M40. This makes the town perfect for the modern way of life, with every type of transport on the doorstep – international travel from Heathrow is just a few miles away, fast trains into London and easy access to the motorway network. Surprisingly, even though it has a population of 13,000, it is still classed as a village, making it one of the largest in England. It also blends into Gerrards Cross to the south, lifting the area to a population of 19,000 people. Here is the main Chiltern Railways line that links London to Birmingham.

It is no surprise that this is another upmarket and exclusive commuter town, with some of the most expensive house prices in England. Despite its Saxon origins, most of the town is of modern architecture with a few Georgian properties remaining.

Nearby is the hamlet of Jordans. This has strong links with the advent of Quakerism in the seventeenth century, continuing the local tradition of non-conformism. In 1687, during the reign of James II, the Declaration of Indulgence was the first step towards religious freedom, enabling new groups to develop. At Jordans a small group, led by William Penn, set up one of the first Friends Meeting Houses. He also travelled and is widely accepted as the founder of Pennsylvania. Nearby is a favourite spot with Americans – the Mayflower Barn, reputed to have been built with timbers from the original *Mayflower* ship.

The area just north of the M40 is the most heavily populated of the Chilterns, from Gerrards Cross, through Beaconsfield and then the nearest thing to a Chiltern capital – High

Wycombe. Beaconsfield was recently cited as "Britain's richest town" with its exceptionally high house prices. This was the first stage coach stop between London and Oxford and boasts an unusually wide main street with attractive red brick buildings, some dating back to Georgian times. Rather like Amersham, the "old" town clusters around the old stagecoach route while the "new" town has developed around the railway, forming a separate centre of its own. This is not far from Hughenden Manor near High Wycombe, which was the home of Benjamin Disraeli, explaining why he was given the title Earl of Beaconsfield. The surrounding hinterland is one of beechwoods with easy public access, including the well-known Burnham Beeches only a few miles to the south. Pinewood Studios are only a few miles away, ensuring that this town and many of the surrounding villages are commonly used as locations, including many of the James Bond films.

The location of Beaconsfield is ideal, being well connected to Heathrow and Slough with the M4 corridor to the south, having the M40 alongside the town and with London only 24 miles away, with direct trains to Marylebone on the Chiltern line. Top businessmen and celebrities are attracted to live here; earlier residents included Enid Blyton and Sir Terry Pratchett was born here. The first ever miniature model village, known as Bekonscot, has developed into a tourist attraction with extension exhibits at a 1/12 scale, including working railways.

Penn lies to the north-west towards High Wycombe. Another popular village for an exclusive address, this is a linear settlement, with a couple of pubs and the church, which is reputedly at such an elevated height that eight counties can be seen from its tower. The Penn estate extends across a swathe of beautiful landscape, with the owners thoughtfully providing a network of well signposted bridleways and footpaths. At the northern extremity of this lies Penn Street, close to the main road to Amersham. The church at Penn Street is full of tombs to the various aristocratic residents of the past and has a rather notorious resident in the churchyard, being the final resting place for the ashes of Donald Maclean, the spy who defected to Moscow in 1951. Segraves Manor was the home to the original Penn family, later to become the Curzon family and in more recent times the Howe family, with Earl Howe still living at Penn. The epitome of an English summer can be experienced at Penn Street with a pint at the Squirrel pub when a cricket match is in full swing on the green opposite.

This leads us to the only really major urban centre in the Chilterns – arguably its *de facto* capital, the town of High Wycombe with its population of 92,000 or 118,000 if we include the surrounding areas. It was, until 1947, a fairly modest town known as Chepping Wycombe. Most of its growth has come since the Second World War; today, most locals refer simply to their town as Wycombe.

High Wycombe lies in a fairly spectacular steep sided river valley – the Wye, a word which itself means combe or valley. The descent by road from the M40 is steep and long, making

The Crown Inn at Penn, a traditional brick built Chiltern pub.

this an unusual setting for a town in the south of England – it feels more like the Yorkshire mill towns or the Welsh coal valleys as you descend towards the town centre. It was certainly occupied by the Romans: a villa has been well excavated with finds in the local museum. The Normans occupied and the town – then known as Wicumun – had its church consecrated in 1087, very soon after the invasion. As with other parts of the Chilterns, the Civil War was very much in evidence, with skirmishes between the two armies.

Although originally a market town, its basis was as the leading manufacturing centre for furniture production in the UK, exporting throughout the world and especially to the former British Empire with its enormous markets. For this reason, its impact on the Chilterns has been enormous as what were once small cottage enterprises coalesced into major companies like Ercol and Parker Knoll, using a ready supply of locally skilled labour with a strong tradition of working with wood over many generations. As the factories grew, so did the demand for the raw materials and the method of production where components were fashioned within the beechwoods where the timber was felled, to then be assembled into the finished product. By 1875, the daily output of chairs was an estimated 4700 units.

With this sudden expansion, terraced housing was built to house the army of workers needed in the factories. Poorly built, these houses rapidly became slums and most were cleared in the early twentieth century; this resulted in new housing that could only expand up the valley sides, creating the urban sprawl that we see today with housing reaching the plateau of the Chilterns several hundred feet above the valley floor. As with most of UK manufacturing, overseas competition with cheap labour has had a devastating impact, with only a few factories remaining today. This created major problems with social deprivation in the 1970s with high unemployment. The town has now recovered, especially with more mobility with better roads and rail networks, and especially with the huge demand for labour at Heathrow airport which is easily accessible.

Wycombe also has strong connections with the RAF, chosen as the Headquarters for RAF Bomber Command in the Second World War; today RAF High Wycombe retains a major strategic role with its own nuclear bunkers. During the Cold War, this would have been of major importance as a centre for logistical command in the event of any atomic attacks. Although not an airbase, it remains a major centre and large employer for the town.

Today, the town is rather typical of so many – a monument to consumerism with sprawling shopping malls and leisure venues. Apart from a few buildings such as the Guildhall, there is little evidence of its Georgian and Victorian past. However, there is an excellent theatre and Wycombe supports its own football team and the Wasps rugby union team.

The local museum is on Priory Avenue at Castle Hill House, a surviving eighteenth century house on a medieval site. The displays and exhibits of chair manufacturing are good, but it is also worth visiting the Living Chair Museum beside the Stewart Linford factory, one

The mausoleum tops the hill overlooking West Wycombe.

of the few remaining specialist factories. The legacy of furniture making has remained and the local Buckinghamshire New University offers specialist courses related to furniture production and design.

The hinterland offers some fairly spectacular options. At the very edge of town lies the choice of two National Trust properties – Hughenden Manor and West Wycombe Park. Both are worthy of a visit.

West Wycombe Park is a 5000 acre area of parkland and lakes to the west of High Wycombe on the old A40 road. Coming from the town, the approach is dominated by the eminence of the mausoleum and St Lawrence's church, perched at the very top of West Wycombe Hill above the village, reminiscent of some Italian scene. Once part of the estate, today the village is largely owned by the National Trust. There are excellent fifteenth century and sixteenth century buildings in the heart of the village itself, with its surviving medieval shops and magnificent village hall. The hill has a long history, offering an excellent defensive site overlooking the confluence of two valleys. It was probably occupied in the Bronze Age and the Romans are also evident – and the imposing mausoleum, built by the Dashwoods, has a distinctly Roman feel. It was also a Saxon village, later known as Haveringdon which was

The medieval Village Hall at West Wycombe.

The caves used by the Hellfire Club.

wiped out in the Black Death. A new village was built in the valley and named West Wycombe – meaning in the valley of the Wye.

The Palladian-style West Wycombe Park mansion is set on the banks of the River Wye in landscaped gardens, with temples that echo those at Stourhead. The estate was established by the infamous Sir Francis Dashwood who founded the Dillettanti Society and the more notorious Hellfire Club. The house was built between 1740 and 1800 and is one of the most Italianate in style to be found in England, making this a favoured location for costume dramas such as *Cranford*. The elegant style is continued throughout the inside, with wonderful frescoes and mementoes from the Grand Tour as Dashwood had a keen interest in classical art. His interest also extended to far more risqué activities, when with friends including William Hogarth he hosted the Hellfire Club deep within the caves, with much wine, women and song. The caves are man-made, in a scheme sponsored by Dashwood to relieve poverty through providing local employment and improve local roads with the materials. Today, the caves are open to the public and are cut deep into the West Wycombe Hill on the opposite side of the valley from the house.

Although the estate is managed by the National Trust, the Dashwood family still own much of it and live in the house, which is closed in the winter months but is used for events, shooting and corporate entertainment.

Within only a few miles to the north east is another great estate, famous for its connection with Benjamin Disraeli – Hughenden Manor. Purchased in 1848, he was forced to borrow the money to pay for it, as leading members of the Conservative Party were expected to have large country properties. Unlike its neighbour, the house is very much a product of the Victorian period, with brickwork and bay windows offering a fine view into the parkland below. The National Trust has restored the gardens to their original glory, notably the walled garden and the formal gardens created by Disraeli's wife, later Lady Beaconsfield. Both are buried in a

Hughenden Manor, the home of Benjamin Disraeli.

vault in the church lying within the estate, down in the valley near the modern entrance for visitors. This church has a unique feature – a special memorial erected by Queen Victoria to honour Disraeli, her greatest confidant, advisor and friend for many years. After service as a centre for analysing aerial photographs during the Second World War, the estate was passed over to the National Trust; internally, there are many exhibits that have been retained since the time of its famous owners. The surrounding parkland of rolling meadows and fine trees provides wonderful access for the local residents in nearby High Wycombe.

North from Hughenden are several linear villages nestling in a landscape of valleys and beechwoods. Walters Ash is the HQ for RAF Strike Command and famous for its nuclear bunker – a far cry from the ancient Grim's Ditch which runs through this area, forming the boundary between the warring tribes around 300BC.

To complete this chapter, we move along the A40 to the west of West Wycombe Park. This road is now much quieter as the nearby M40 takes all the burden of the traffic from the north through the Chilterns to London. The village of Stokenchurch is the last settlement before

Opposite: *The parkland valley below Hughenden with its church.*

Summer in the beechwoods near Stokenchurch.

reaching the scarp of the hills above Aston Rowant, where the M40 descends to the Vale of Oxford through its spectacular chalk cutting. Being sited at the top of the steep climb on the old main road, this was a natural resting place to refresh horses on the journey to London. As a result it held some strategic importance and was a flashpoint during the Civil War, with regular skirmishes recorded between the Royalist forces, based in Oxford to the north, and the Parliamentarians based in London to the south. King Charles is reputed to have stayed at the Kings Hotel during this period. This area of the scarp was very active during the Civil War and the local population paid a heavy price with reprisals and sackings a regular occurrence.

The area is heavily wooded, and had a strong tradition of furniture making with its own factories in the past, in addition to feeding the raw materials along the toll road to Wycombe only seven miles to the east. For walkers, the route along one of the original roads, a bridleway known today as Colliers Lane, provides a wonderful walk through lovely beech woods interspersed with rolling farmland towards Radnage and Bledlow Ridge.

For any travellers taking the M40 towards Oxford, a diversion at the junction for Stokenchurch is rewarded with almost instant access to the most beautiful countryside. To the north is a landscape of great charm with wonderful walking and secluded valleys. To the south, the road immediately becomes quite rural, leading into an idyllic landscape of the best Chiltern traditions – chalk and trees. This area around Ibsden is just the start of the area covered by the next chapter.

Opposite: Colliers Lane near Stoken-church was once a major route through this area.

Autumn hedgerow at Penn.

The dry valley at Radnage, near Stokenchurch.

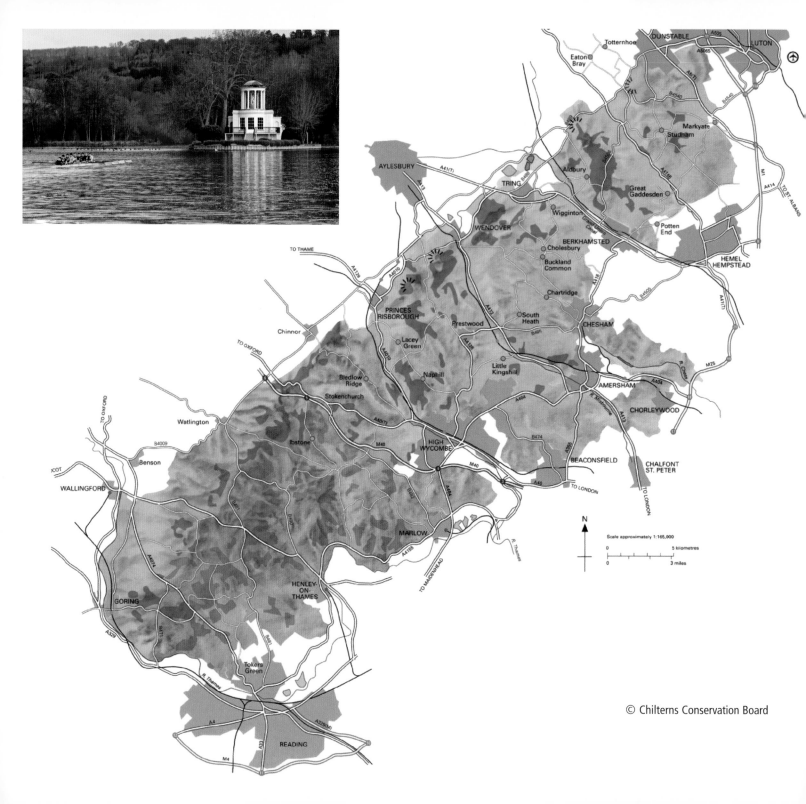

DUNSTABLE
Totternhoe
LUTON
Eaton
Bray
Markyate
Studham
A505
A5(T)
B4540
A4146
A414
TO ST ALBANS
M1
AYLESBURY
A41(T)
TRING
Aldbury
Great
Gaddesden
Potten
End
HEMEL
HEMPSTEAD
A41(T)
WENDOVER
Wigginton
BERKHAMSTED
Cholesbury
Buckland
Common
Chartridge
A413
M25
TO THAME
A4129
PRINCES
RISBOROUGH
Prestwood
South
Heath
CHESHAM
A41
Chinnor
A4010
Lacey
Green
Naphill
Little
Kingshill
R. Chess
AMERSHAM
A404
TO OXFORD
Bledlow
Ridge
Stokenchurch
A4128
CHORLEYWOOD
A413
Watlington
A40(T)
Ibstone
M40
HIGH
WYCOMBE
A404
BEACONSFIELD
CHALFONT
ST. PETER
B4009
Benson
M40
B474
A40
TO LONDON
TO LONDON
XCOT
WALLINGFORD
MARLOW
A4155
TO MAIDENHEAD
R. Thames
N

Scale approximately 1:165,000

0   5 kilometres
0   3 miles

GORING
HENLEY-
ON-
THAMES
A329
A4074
B481
Tokers
Green
R. Thames
A4
A329(M)
READING
M4
A33

© Chilterns Conservation Board

CHAPTER FOUR
THE SOUTH CHILTERNS AND DOWN TO THE THAMES

To the south of the M40 the pattern of the landscape differs from the northern Chilterns. In place of the large towns and small hamlets of the northern area, we now enter a landscape of small villages, clustered around the church and village hall. Most of these are at a relatively high altitude, often over 200 metres above sea level, set in glorious countryside of valleys and offering one of the most densely wooded landscapes in southern England. These valleys tend to drift in a north-south direction, many being dry, towards the River Thames between Marlow in the east and around to Goring in the west. Here the Thames takes a dramatic loop around the Chilterns, turning south through the Goring Gap and then swinging round to the east at Pangbourne and on through Reading before turning north again after Sonning and up to Henley-on-Thames. The steep hills come right down to the banks of the Thames throughout this stretch, particularly at Whitchurch and Caversham. This close relationship between the hill and the valley has resulted in this area being often connected as the "Thames and Chilterns" as they form part of the same landscape. This chapter dips its toe into the river as well, as it cannot depict the Chilterns without acknowledging the influence of the Thames.

As before, this is a chalk landscape with occasional drifts of overlying clay that were used for brick making. The villages rely on bringing water up through wells as the few rivers are unreliable in dry weather; the lack of regular rivers, as we have seen to the north, has spared this area from the invasion of road and railways. Many villages still have their Victorian wells, long out of use but a reminder of former times; it is also common to find that larger houses also had wells to tap the water table in the chalk. In wet weather, the valleys can spring to life again and clear streams chatter down through the meadows and after extreme rainfall events the overfull streams join into larger watercourses and can even cause flooding lower down, as at Henley on occasion. The lack of water explains why these higher villages developed at a later time, when compared to those along the spring-line. There is evidence of earlier habitation when water was readily available in places like Hambleden with its recently discovered Roman settlement.

The economy developed from early agriculture and the raw materials from the extensive woodland available for charcoal burning and timber for furniture making. The growth of large towns in the Victorian period spawned a great demand for building materials and food, particularly for Reading and London. Old droving routes were used to drive livestock down to the market in Reading and then on by train to London; most of these have evolved as the roads we use today, but some droves still survive as footpaths but have echoes of a more important function to justify their scale. These also explain the wonderful deep lanes, sometimes called holloways, that often link the villages. These can cut deep below the surrounding fields, rather like the bocage of Normandy, with beech trees flanking the route. As a result this is superb walking country with a veritable network of footpaths and bridleways that can offer beechwoods, valleys, wildlife and the local pub in shortish routes. The local guides to walks from pubs are very useful as a quick and easy option and are invariably good and varied. This myriad of tracks is also heaven for mountain biking, to the annoyance of some

A typical lane through woods at Christmas Common.

walkers – and this is also big time horse country.

This area is prized for its unspoilt countryside. It is hard to imagine when walking in this area that London is only a short distance away and the bustling town of Reading within only a few miles. This is particularly evident in the hills overlooking Mapledurham; the Chilterns have retained their character, forming a bastion to the urban sprawl immediately south of the Thames in suburban Reading.

Much of this unique character is down to local political boundaries. The boundary for Oxfordshire follows the Thames; this means that the huge growth of Berkshire has been

restricted to the south of the river. As a consequence, there are regular demands by Berkshire for the boundary to be shifted to the north, to enable further development for Reading into the Chilterns. Unsurprisingly, this is fiercely resisted and any proposed boundary changes have been rebuffed at the regular Boundary Commission reviews but there will continue to be this threat. To the credit of Oxfordshire County Council, the South Chilterns have been carefully managed and any major development of new towns has been prevented and the AONB designation respected. When crossing the Thames from Berkshire into Oxfordshire, the difference is immediately evident – one is leaving a heavily built up area and entering a beautiful landscape of fields and woods.

The area is defined to the north by the M40 and otherwise broadly by the course of the Thames. This is quite a special area of the Chilterns, as the geography has worked in its favour. Unlike the northern Chilterns, there are no major communication routes as there are no valleys cutting through to connect the Thames Valley with the north. Consequently this leaves the area very unspoilt, with quiet lanes and small villages with the only two main routes being the old toll road from Henley to Oxford, nowadays the A4130 and the A4074 which connects Reading to Oxford. With these exceptions, the Chilterns of South Oxfordshire feature a myriad network of small roads connecting hamlets and villages, usually following ancient droving routes that often pass through magnificent beechwoods. In spring these provide some of the best bluebell

woods and then come into glorious colour again in the autumn when the trees turn to gold. The area is therefore very unspoilt with no major development; step out at night and the clear sky is evidence of no light pollution as the major towns are far enough away.

This part of our exploration begins close to the M40 and then takes us southwards, often down long dry valleys that will eventually meet the Thames. In addition there are several hill villages that emerged through agriculture and woodworking, or occasional brick manufacturing. As we can see elsewhere, the story is now very different with cottages fetching high prices for those working in Reading or taking the journey into London. However, there are no convenient stations as the main line comes through the Goring Gap down to Reading and then into Paddington, with branch lines to Henley and Marlow. It is therefore essential to have a car to get to the station and this has led to some congestion at peak hours, especially at the pinch points where the bridges cross the Thames. Rush hour in Henley or Caversham is best avoided.

Using the boundary of the Area of Outstanding Beauty as the best guide, the first place to explore is the small village of Lane End, very close to the M40 and High Wycombe. This

Opposite: The Oxfordshire Way passes down into Bix Bottom.

Far left: *In May, the bluebell woods are magnificent.*

Left: *Dawn sunlight in the beechwoods near Checkendon.*

Brick and flint cottages at Turville.

makes this an attractive location for those working in Wycombe looking for a rural retreat within easy reach, or needing a convenient link to the motorway. What is immediately typical of the area is the elevation above sea level at 200 metres, high enough to feel the worst effects of any winter weather. The traditional agricultural speciality was barley for the breweries in Marlow and Henley, together with the usual woodworking for the furniture factories nearby. Today, it has attracted small light industrial estates because of its accessibility to the road networks and, for the same reason, conference centres. At weekends the attractive local pubs can get busy with walkers that come to the area to enjoy the many good routes, especially down into the Hambleden Valley and where they can watch the many red kites at close quarters. In this area you may see other things in flight, as this is close to the Booker airfield which lies just east of Lane End. This is a much favoured gliding centre and it is very common to see elegant gliders being towed by light aircraft to gain height before jettisoning the tow cables.

The landscape immediately south of the M40, going west, is remarkably unspoilt – except for the constant rumble of the traffic, that can be heard from some distance. This is where some of the long dry valleys start their journey towards the Thames, still some six miles away. Stokenchurch and Ibstone sit on the ridge between two of these valleys. The first of these twists and turns through steep sides, through a totally unspoilt landscape to join the Hamble Brook just below the village of Fingest. As with so much of this area, the entire valley can be walked, from Stokenchurch and the motorway to Fingest, some four miles of the finest Chilterns. It is hard to imagine that one is so close to such a major highway and that this is scarcely thirty miles from London. It is utterly unspoilt with wonderful beechwoods, steep sided pastures and is criss-crossed by an extensive network of other paths leading to Ibstone, Cadmore End and Turville. Much of this is down to stewardship, as this is the country of large estates and a large investment in shooting. Winter walks may require care as it is easy to stumble into one of the many shoots by mistake – although there are usually diversions provided to avoid any danger.

Winter woods after a shower.

Harvest time in the Stonor Valley.

101

The ridge is the site of Ibstone, not to be confused with Ipsden further to the west. This linear village, follows the road that links Junction 5 of the M40 down to the Hambleden Valley. This is unusual as it is really only a narrow lane that shares the junction with Stokenchurch. Of course this makes the village highly desirable as it offers almost immediate access to the motorway and then into London. As a consequence, once simple cottages have been extended into highly desirable homes with fantastic views across the valley below, alongside larger country houses such as Ibstone House. The village straddles the boundary between Oxfordshire and Buckinghamshire – and most of the southern Chilterns fall within what is politically defined as "South Oxfordshire". The church is very old, probably Saxon but with even earlier importance – this is set apart from the village and sits on a shelf overlooking the Turville Valley to the west. The study of gravestones can be interesting and here you can find the epitaph to a "racing driver and aviator" which conjures up wonderful images of earlier days. Around here, red kites are so common that they are with you for most of any walk – the author recently counted seventeen red kites in one tree at Ibstone!

This area is cricket country. The stereotypical scene of the English countryside, with the local team in white flannels being served local beer by the pub that looks over the green is very much part of South Oxfordshire. The cricket club has been an important centre of social life for most of the past century and this tradition continues with local leagues. Ibsden has a lively cricket team that was the 2009 champion in the local 20/20 league. It is a healthy sign of changing times to note that these days some of the key players are called Khan, Patel and Saeed, alongside names like Carruthers and Smith.

Ibstone Church, of Saxon origins, overlooks the Hambleden Valley.

The Cobstone Windmill overlooks the Hambleden Valley at Turville.

The most notable feature of Ibstone is the excellent windmill – which is really overlooking Turville and is some way south of the village on the lane that leads to Fingest. Called Cobstone Windmill and built in 1816, it is a twelve sided smock mill which is now a private residence. There is a footpath that runs close by which enables a reasonable view. Devotees of the television comedy *The Vicar of Dibley* will instantly recognise that the view from here down to Turville is used for the opening sequence shots for the series. Until 1967 it had fallen into dereliction, but was rescued as the site for Caractacus Pott's workshop in *Chitty Chitty Bang Bang* and is where the flying car is filmed taking to the skies. Although only partially renovated for the film, it was purchased by the actor Hayley Mills and converted into a private residence.

The second great dry valley runs down the western side of the Ibstone ridge. This runs from the very edge of the M40 and then through the Wormsley Estate, wending its way eventually to Turville before merging into the Hambeldon Valley. As before, this is exceptional walking country with rolling, fulsome slopes with beechwoods and pastures. Almost the entire valley until Turville is managed as part of the Wormsley Estate, owned by the Getty family in recent years. The main valley footpath offers a sudden surprise: in the middle of this perfect valley lies Wormsley Park but in the foreground, but not accessible from the path, is the most perfect cricket pitch – Sir Paul Getty's Ground – with its thatched pavilion. J. Paul Getty Junior was an Anglophile who, unusually for an American, mastered an understanding and love of cricket. He was persuaded by Mick Jagger to build a replica of The Oval in 1992. With sufficient wealth to create his own first-class ground, this remarkable location hosted The Queen Mother and John Major at the inaugural match. Today, it is a major

Turville cottages and the Cobstone Windmill.

Autumn woods near Wormsley.

Fallow deer herd in the upper Hambleden Valley.

cricket venue hosting several major matches – including the women's Test Matches between England and Australia. It is a favourite location for many well-known cricketers and overseas tourists for warm up matches against the MCC. More recently, the estate has hosted the annual Garsington Opera season as well.

Wormsley also played a key role in the re-establishment of the red kite in the 1990s. Young chicks were brought from northern Spain over a period of three years. After an acclimatisation period in large cages in the beech woods at Wormsley, they were gradually released into the wild. This has proved to be one to most successful projects of its type and is now being replicated elsewhere – with chicks from the Chilterns. From these small beginnings, in total 96 pairs, there are now well over 1000 pairs and the area for red kites increases every year, to the extent that they have now been sighted over London and well into Wiltshire. These birds seem quite happy in urban areas as well and can be seen over Reading and Wallingford town centres regularly – much to excitement of any visiting twitchers who may happen to be parking in the local supermarket.

This valley is a perfect day out, with pubs to look forward to at Turville or Christmas Common. Apart from the private road up to the house, there are no other roads at all – just

Superb autumn colours near Christmas Common.

the bridleway and a myriad of connecting paths. One recommended route is to leave the car at Cowleaze Wood close to the M40 cutting, and take the path down the Wormsley Valley and then on a circular route through Christmas Common with its welcome Fox and Hounds pub. As well as the red kites, there are other raptors to see and many deer in the surrounding woods; in autumn the colours are spectacular.

From Wormsley the track meets the narrow lane that runs down to Turville, known as the "Holloway" and running between high steep banks under an archway of beech trees. This small lane is beautiful in any season, but it really comes into its own in spring. Then the beech trees have just come into leaf and have that new green colour that is so fresh, offset by the most wonderful bluebells as one approaches the village. It is just perfect, which is probably why it was chosen for a memorable scene in the TV drama *Goodnight Mr Tom* when the evacuee boy William was learning to ride his bike.

Turville is quite small, with its brick and flint cottages and Bull and Butcher pub overlooked by the Cobstone Windmill high above. This is, rather like the cricket, almost too English, to the extent that it is a favourite for the film and television industry – especially being so close to the studios at Pinewood. This is Dibley – used for the BBC comedy series with Dawn French as the lady vicar. Turville Park, the large estate overlooking the village to the west, is the country home of Lord Sainsbury and the famous playwright John Mortimer had his family home at nearby Turville Heath.

The two valleys meet just south of Fingest to form the Hambleden Valley. Fingest is another village of ancient origins with its old Norman church, which has an unusual double vaulted roof. It is interesting that the derivation of its name refers to "wooded hill where wooden assemblies are made" which may suggest that the idea of furniture components may go back a very long time. Local tradition cites that there is a ghost in Fingest – The Green Man – that is of Bishop Henry Burghersh who took land from local people in the fourteenth century causing great hardship. His spirit attempts to assuage his guilt by seeking forgiveness. For visitors there is also a welcome break at the Chequers pub opposite the church.

The Holloway Lane above Turville in early spring.

The village of Turville from Cobstone Windmill.

The Norman church at Fingest, with its unusual tower.

Opposite: *An old barn in the Hambleden Valley.*

The Hambleden Valley is another wonderful area. To climb Turville Hill and look down the valley to the south opens a vista of woods and small hamlets, leading eventually to the Thames below Hambleden. The valley floor here is evidently wetter, with the dry stream springing to life in winter or after heavy rain. In fact, Water Lane running south of Turville has now been closed to traffic, as it became so prone to occasional flooding. Despite this, the stream is still just a trickle when compared to the scale of the valley itself. It is intriguing to wonder at how these large valleys came into being. They are dry, unless there has been exceptional rainfall and yet the scale of the valleys would suggest much more serious origins. It is probable that they owe their origin to the Ice Age, as channels for meltwater from the great ice sheets. It is hard to comprehend that this ice was a mile thick, suggesting that massive amounts of water must have flowed from the receding ice sheets during the Ice Age.

The valley runs through Skirmett, another brick and flint row of cottages that were once poor but more likely – today – to have a Porsche in the lane outside. Only a few years ago, this tiny village once had three pubs; today there is The Frog and the other two have reverted to residential use. Invariably these South Oxfordshire pubs belong to Brakspears Brewery, until recently based at Henley-on-Thames. Although no longer actually brewed in Henley, Brakspears is a much loved beer that evokes many affectionate and probably hazy memories

for generations of young oarsmen attending the Henley Regatta and retains its popularity. Walking is the main activity around here and at weekends the pub will fill with hearty souls asked to leave their muddy boots in the porch while they crave a well-deserved pub lunch. Nearby is the Chiltern Valley Winery, also known as Luxters located up a narrow lane through beech woods. This is a successful micro-brewery and vineyard producing some wonderful wines, notably white wines that have won many prizes – 120,000 bottles are produced annually. Visitors can arrange to join tours and there is a shop that allows tastings and offers a good range of options. The beers are unusual in that they are fermented within the bottle – rather like champagne.

Farms dot the valley floor – Arizona Farm, Colstrope Farm and The Hyde – all with old barns and traditional buildings that speak of an earlier age in farming. Cattle farming does well in the valley floor and some of these farms have maintained that tradition, but it is becoming increasingly rare owing to the economic pressures. Arable and sheep farming are now more common land uses, with a high population of grazing set aside for horses, as the Hambleden Valley is very popular for its equestrian facilities.

As is so often the case in the Chilterns, certain families are closely linked to particular villages. This is the case at Hambleden, linked over many generations with the Smith family, of the W.H. Smith empire. Hambleden Manor was recently sold, ending this link. Hambleden, like its neighbour Turville, as more famous for being a film set these days. Visitors will tour the area to see where this film or that TV series was set – there are even special tours now for *Midsomer Murder* locations. The church is fourteenth century and includes some fine memorials to the D'Oyley family and the ornate ceiling is very beautiful. The village, primarily of brick and flint cottages with dormer windows, is a firm favourite for TV film crews and the shops are used to represent the "typical" English village of the mid twentieth century. One property, once the bakery but now a private house, has retained its "Hovis" bread logo above the original shop façade. The village was actually used as a base for US troops in the build-up to D-Day in 1944, so it was a fitting location for *Band of Brothers* to depict that period.

Immediately south of the village is evidence of substantial Roman settlements. Recent archaeological investigations have unearthed a great mystery. The remains of 97 infants were found in a mass burial. All were of the same age and the expert opinion is that infanticide was not uncommon in Roman times and that unwanted infants in the circumstances of a brothel would simply be disposed of. This rather unpalatable conclusion is the only explanation, to date, for such an unusual find.

To fully appreciate Hambleden and its setting, it is recommended to use the car park to the south and then walk along the footpath across the water meadows up to the village, with the Manor House on the slopes behind. Once in the village, its charm is immediate and one

The village of Skirmett, once a poor farming village but affluent today.

The old butchers shop at Hambleden, no longer in use other than useful backdrop for films.

Hambleden Church.

can see why it is such a favoured location. There is a thriving village store that also serves coffee. After some refreshment at the Stag and Huntsman, retrace your route but stay on the road down to Hambleden Lock.

This is an important moment in our exploration. The Chilterns meet the Thames at last. Take care crossing the main road between Marlow and Henley and take the small footpath towards the river. At first this passes through a passageway before opening up with the wonderful view of Hambleden Lock, with water noisily rushing over the weir. To the right is the old mill, now turned into rather exclusive apartments. Follow the path across the weir and to the lock itself – a gem of a Thames lock. This is likely to be scene of some activity in summer months as various boats of different shapes and sizes bump and slide their way in and out of the lock. Floating gin palaces dwarf the odd skiff, while the lovely narrow boats add a

Another old shop now used as a private residence but retaining its useful period branding.

bit of style. Looking back from the river, one can see just how intimate the Chilterns are here – the hills come right down to the Thames itself and the landscape is not just of the Thames as the river and the hills are cheek by jowl. This is already very close to the Henley reach which is so famous as the regatta course – this is a wonderful way to approach Henley via the riverside if walking a few miles is no object. Shortly upstream from Hambleden Lock is a wonderful riverside property on the northern bank of the river, with sweeping lawns and cedar trees. This is Greenlands, once another home for the Smith family but now the Henley Management College which is part of Reading University.

We continue the theme of valleys by returning back into the hills and starting from Christmas Common, visited in the first chapter. From here, another valley system starts – the Stonor Valley – another significant dry valley that runs all the way to Henley. From the high

Anglers try their luck at Hambleden Lock.

valley the well-marked Oxfordshire Way passes through unspoilt and remote countryside. This leads through lovely beechwoods which were until quite recently used for charcoal burning, through a few farms to eventually join the Stonor Valley at Pishill. This is only a small hamlet with a lovely church which is set on the valley side and contains a wonderful modern stain glass window by John Piper who once lived nearby. The Crown Inn includes a thatched barn which is often used as a wedding venue and is reputed to have once been a refuge for Catholics during the Reformation, especially given its proximity to Stonor.

The jewel of this valley is Stonor House, set in very beautiful parkland with its own herd of fallow deer. The setting for this house is just perfect, slightly elevated above the valley road but in its own side valley, surrounded by beech woods that form a bowl within which sits this wonderful building. This has been described as "possibly the most beautiful setting for any house in England" by the late Lord Gibson who had been Chairman of the National Trust; it is also much admired by Simon Jenkins in his book on *England's Thousand Best Houses*. Taking the footpath that rises up the hillside to the south of the house, one can see just how perfect it is, with its own chapel to one side, its walled Italianate gardens and sweeping driveway. The same family – the Stonors – have lived continuously at Stonor for over 850 years with the present owners being Lord and Lady Camoys. The house, which is open to the public in the summer months, is of considerable architectural interest, probably originally built in the late twelfth century. It is sited next to a pre-historic stone circle which can still be seen in the lawns to the front of the house. Internally, it contains very fine collections of tapestries, rare paintings and other art works collected over the centuries

Stonor is perhaps most famous for its resistance to the religious oppression of the sixteenth

Greenlands, now the Henley Management College.

Folds in the fields near Pishill.

Stonor House, in its beautiful valley setting surrounded by parkland and beech woods.

century, stoically remaining Catholic to this day – the chapel is still used for mass every week. The resistance during this period included offering sanctuary to many, including Edmund Campion before he was arrested and then hung, drawn and quartered on 1st December 1581. Despite periods of imprisonment, the Stonors managed to hold on to their beliefs and allowed their chapel to be a haven to other Catholics in the area. Visitors to the house will be shown the "Priest Hole" where the recusants were hidden during the various raids, together with an exhibition about the sanctified St Edmund Campion.

In the spring the gardens are a delight, with wonderful collections which include exotic specimens. Behind the house are a series of walled gardens in an Italian style, with ponds, terraces, ancient yews and a Japanese-style summer house. The old kitchen garden has been converted into a host of flower beds, and in May there are swathes of daffodils and narcissi on the hillside above. The grounds are often used to host events in the summer months, with craft fairs, events for VW enthusiasts and spectacular outdoor concerts with famous artists now a regular local attraction on the events calendar.

On the hills above the Stonor Valley there is a patchwork of beech woods and open pasture, usually for sheep grazing. Small hamlets of flint and brick cottages, sometimes with a small pub now surviving through good food rather than beer, dot the landscape. At Maidensgrove

Winter in the beech woods near Pishill.

113

is one of the larger commons to be found in this part of the Chilterns – an area of open land that extends as far as Russell's Water. In the summer months local families come here to fly kites and have picnics in grassland that still harbours some wild flowers. Between Maidensgrove and Bix is one of the finest nature reserves in the Chilterns – the Warburg Nature Reserve which is operated by the Berkshire, Buckinghamshire and Oxfordshire Wildlife Trust (BBOWT). The reserve covers most of the valley known locally as Bix Bottom, with a mixture of species rich chalk grassland and ancient woodland, offering high levels of biodiversity. Over 2000 different species of plant, butterfly, animal and fungus have been recorded. The chalk grassland supports several species of orchid in summer. A visit enables a glimpse of the natural state that might have been typical of the Chilterns before the advent of modern farming and forestry practices. As usual, the red kites are almost constant companions, but there are also many buzzards, owls and other rare species of bird to be found. There is an excellent visitor centre near the car park with well marked routes to follow – sometimes there are organised events such as fungus forays, so it is worth checking the website for information before any planned visits.

Opposite: The prehistoric stone circle at Stonor, with the Stonor Valley below.

The main valley at Stonor.

A misty morning in the Warburg Nature Reserve at Bix.

Below: *Fawley Court, beside the Thames near Henley.*

To the east of the valley – on the watershed between the Stonor and the Hambleden valleys, is another small hamlet, Fawley. Devotees of rowing will be familiar as "Fawley" represents an early stage on the regatta course. This is misleading as the hamlet is actually two miles from the river, but the reference is probably derived from Fawley Court, which does sit beside the river opposite Remenham, another well-known name to oarsmen. Fawley itself is a linear settlement high above the surrounding valleys. The village includes several beautiful houses that were once large farms, often dedicated to horses these days. St Mary's church is another where one can see a stained glass window by the artist John Piper, who lived at Fawley Bottom. There is also a unique feature here – a full scale steam railway with a proper station. This has been built by Sir William McAlpine at his estate, together with a large collection of steam artefacts, with the track passing around his grounds and through the woods. Although a private collection, the railway is occasionally open to the public for charity events, but is not visible from the road, so the occasional whistle at weekends is not another red kite.

Fawley Court is on an ancient site and was a manor long before the Norman invasion, believed to date back to Edward the Confessor. During the Civil War there were skirmishes at Fawley that resulted in the building being sacked. It was rebuilt in 1684 in the style of Wren, creating a perfect symmetrical house set back from the Thames with gardens that were later landscaped by Capability Brown. In recent times it has had various owners, following requisitioning during the Second World War. Until recently it was owned by a Polish religious group – The Marian Fathers – but has now passed back into private ownership. The best view of the house is to take the footpath northwards from Henley along the west bank of the river, from the Phyllis Court Club. Further downstream, on an island set in the centre of the river, a folly was built as part of this estate – Temple Island. Designed by James Wyatt, this is built in an Etruscan style and is now a famous Henley landmark marking the start of the Henley Regatta course. Today, it is managed by the Henley Royal Regatta and is often used as a wedding venue or for occasional private parties.

Moving back into the hills behind Henley, we come into the lower part of the Stonor Valley, to Middle Assendon and Lower Assendon. These are small hamlets that were predominantly farms although there was a significant sawmill until the 1960s. There are two pubs – The Rainbow and the Golden Ball, which lies very close to the old toll road from Oxford to Henley with its mail coaches. These are reputed to have stopped at the Golden Ball – the "Tantivy" from Birmingham, the "Magnet" from Cheltenham and the Gloucester and Stroud mails. This is an area steeped in speculation about the famous highwayman Dick Turpin, who was reputed to operate in the Chilterns. Several pubs, including the Golden Ball, lay claim to having provided sanctuary to Turpin when he was on the run; rather like Campion, he met a sticky end.

The Assendons are at the lowest part of the Stonor Valley, where the stream follows a

Dragon boats race on the Thames at Temple Island.

parallel course with the main road from Oxford, the A4130. The approach to Henley-on-Thames can be on foot or by car. The walk involves taking the lane towards Fawley and then turning into Henley Park. This provides a high level path through parkland above the Thames with glorious views across Hambleden Lock and down the Thames Valley, before descending through beech woods into the town. The car route is equally attractive, following the A4130 along a mile long stretch known as the "Fair Mile" – a fitting description as this is a broad avenue of trees, many being oak planted to celebrate Queen Victoria's Golden Jubilee, flanked with old cottages, still set in a deep valley and forming a perfect approach to Henley. To the east are the woods of Henley Park and to the west there is Lambridge Wood and then Victorian villas, mostly converted to offices, with more beech woods above. In 2001, after extremely heavy rainfall, the springs in the upper Stonor Valley broke to the surface and the Fairmile was deluged, with much damage – it seems that this usually benign stream has an occasional habit of turning into a torrent.

The Golden Ball at Lower Assendon on the old stage coach route to Oxford.

Although it is usual to think of Henley as a Thames town, it is very much a Chiltern town as well. The hills close right in to the Thames, with the steep Greys Hill immediately behind the Town Hall to the west, Henley Park to the north and the equally steep Remenham Hill in the direction of Maidenhead and London, which is actually in Berkshire once over the river. The architecture is definitely Chiltern, being an abundance of brick and flint with charming old mews tucked away. To take the riverside footpath from Henley Bridge towards Hambleden

lock provides a good perspective of Henley. This path is surfaced and very popular for locals to exercise themselves and their dogs, invariably labradors of various shapes and colours. In addition there are the rowing coaches on their bicycles, so intent on watching and shouting at their crews on the river that they are a distinct danger to unaware walkers. Locals know about this and take it for granted, gently giving way but visitors are much more at risk! The river is often a hive of activity with three rowing clubs in action, training all year round. This walk is without doubt one of the finest to be had, with wonderful views of the Chilterns forming a natural amphitheatre as the river swings around to the east towards Hurley.

Beside the river is the old Henley Brewery complex, now redeveloped into very expensive apartments and an exclusive hotel. On the opposite bank is the world famous Leander Rowing Club, where famous oarsmen such as Pinsent and Redgrave trained for the Olympics; it is usual to see oarsmen training from here with their unusual pink colours – officially known as cerise.

The town exudes wealth – in 2010 the most expensive town in England in terms of housing cost, outside of London. Exclusive restaurants, designer coffee shops and specialist fashion shops sit alongside the more mundane high street names. The Town Hall dominates the market place, which is pedestrianised and offers a pleasant place to eat al fresco in the summer months. However, the greatest jewel in Henley is the most elegant of all bridges across the Thames – its five arches supporting the gently elevated curve formed by the bridge itself. Anyone familiar with Henley would recognise its profile immediately, as there are few other bridges quite like this for sheer style. The bridge is overlooked by the church of St Mary, with its tower dominating the riverside and offering, for those lucky enough to get access, the best view up the course of the Henley Regatta. Beside the church are beautiful almshouses and

Opposite: *The Fairmile is an elegant approach into Henley from Oxford.*

The famous Leander Rowing Club at Henley.

Oarsmen are usually training on the river at Henley.

the chantry is often open in summer. Old streets, such as Friday Street, provide a glimpse of medieval Henley, with some surviving Tudor houses.

Any visit to Henley should include a trip to the River and Rowing Museum. Opened in 1998 and awarded the UK National Heritage Museum of the Year in 1999, the beautiful modern building contains numerous fixed exhibitions that relate to the development of the sport of rowing, the history of Henley and a special feature on Wind in the Willows which is of great charm and entrances children of all ages. In addition, there are temporary exhibitions which are always of the highest standard. The Kenton Theatre is the fourth oldest working theatre in the country, a survivor from Regency times. This is run entirely by volunteers and is well supported by the local community. The ready supply of celebrities, notably John Mortimer in the past, that live locally and with a willingness to help out certainly helps.

In addition to its fame for the Regatta, the town has recently developed a strong reputation as a centre for the arts. Its location, within easy reach by car and rail from London, makes this the perfect venue for various festivals. The most notable of these is the Henley Festival in July, which attracts international stars with its floating stage in the grounds of what was the Stewards Enclosure at the Regatta during the preceding week. The Henley Literary Festival is gaining momentum and is very popular, supported by local residents such as Jeremy Paxman. In late summer, the river bank is also the venue for other festivals, including Rewind and the Traditional Boat Rally.

For the many thousands of oarsmen and oarswomen across the world, the word "Henley" usually conjures warm memories of the annual Henley Royal Regatta. Steeped in tradition, obsessed by protocol and a huge consumption of Pimms, this is a time warp. Henley Regatta is Edwardian England, where "gentlemen" wear outrageous striped blazers, pink (cerise) socks and schoolboy caps; the "ladies" have a strict dress code to maintain standards. The pecking order is defined by which badge is worn – top dogs are the actual Stewards with their own metal badge, then the Leander badge, a Stewards Enclosure badge, the Remenham Club, Phyllis Court or, heaven forbid, just a General Enclosure badge; below this and it's a picnic on the bank. The format has been set and has created its own sub-culture; old rowing hands will understand the plummy commentary of each race as reference is made to Fawley, The Barrier, Remenham and "approaching the Stewards" and "the current rate of striking". Past oarsman, now portly, gather into reunions for picnic lunches in the car parks, with hampers of smoked salmon and champagne in the boot of the Bentley, reminiscing about old races from days long gone. One paradox is that there are many overseas crews at Henley who must seriously believe that this is representative of England and the English, not realising that this event is culturally unique. The other paradox is the lack of interest in the rowing – Henley is much more a social occasion, with corporate hospitality rampant, than a sporting event and there is far more attention to networking than there is to any river activity. For all its eccentricity, it is a

Within the Stewards Enclosure at Henley Royal Regatta.

Above right: *Beside the Regatta course, looking towards the finish near Henley Bridge.*

wonderful occasion and the colours and atmosphere during the first week of July are memorable. On a fine day, the spectacle looking from the riverside on the town side directly up the course towards Temple Island with the Chilterns beyond, with crews on the water and the light playing on the river is wonderful.

Henley also has a very interesting history. The first record of a bridge was in 1234 and this would have been an important development in linking the south Chilterns towards London. The town itself dates back to pre-Norman times, but it really developed is current form in the thirteenth century having previously been a small hamlet attached to Benson. By the time of the Tudors, Henley was a well established town and had developed as a trading centre with its own market, although it was particularly badly ravaged by the Black Death, losing 60% of its population. What is less well known is that Henley was a very important inland port, servicing goods all the way to London. In addition to transporting food and livestock from the Chiltern farms, there were bricks and tiles from Nettlebed, local glass making factories, brewing and malt, corn and wool merchants. This enabled the town to develop enormous wealth and strategic importance throughout the Middle Ages, explaining in some part the high quality of the architecture. In the nineteenth century this was also the main route for many mail coaches, enabling good access to London for the business community.

This wealth was maintained into the modern era with the development of the railway link to Brunel's Great Western Railway at Twyford. This enabled easy access to London with the wealthy classes able to enjoy the elegance of homes beside the Thames. Today, the motorway network provides good access, although Henley itself can be congested as all the main roads pinch into the bridge, so at peak times Remenham Hill and the town centre can become very busy. The town retains a very pleasant atmosphere and is well worth a visit to savour the river and its elegant surroundings.

Our route from Henley now takes us into a new area, defined by the A4130 to the north and the Thames to the south, as it loops from Wallingford and then down to Reading and back up to Henley. This is an area that is densely wooded with small villages, generally at higher altitude being mostly around 200 metres above sea level. Although close to Reading and Henley, there are only minor roads and small lanes, creating a sense of peace and quiet in an area for outstanding walking. Here the Chilterns remain close to the river and almost step into Reading itself at Caversham, where another long dry valley follows from Cane End to the north. Between Whitchurch and Mapledurham, rolling hills plunge down to the valley within less than a mile from Reading and the main railway line to the west, itself then passing into the narrow defile of the Goring Gap. This close juxtaposition of unspoilt country and town is unusual.

Old medieval houses in Henley.

The villages in this part of South Oxfordshire mostly evolved as agricultural communities servicing the nearby towns of Henley, Reading and Wallingford – and London by boat via Henley and by rail in later times. Many of these villages are given the title "Common" – we have Nettlebed Common, Peppard Common, Sonning Common, Bix Common and Gallowstree Common. These were linked by droves, down into Reading, to drive livestock into the market. In time, these droves became metalled and today form the framework of roads although in places a few remain as bridleways today. As recently as the 1950s many of these lanes were still not surfaced – a recent conversation with a former evacuee from London confirmed his astonishment that the remote muddy lane he recalled from 1940 had changed beyond recognition.

Owing to their location away from the spring-line, water supply was a critical issue. It is interesting that many villages have a pond – some of these are natural and some are man made near a ready supply of fresh water. In pre-Victorian times these ponds would have played a key role but were generally replaced by communal well systems in the Victorian era. These remain in many cases and a quick search will still lead to the well, thankfully preserved and protected although no longer used. The most spectacular of these is at Stoke Row, which is featured at more length later in this chapter.

The Victorian well at Kidmore End.

Rising from Lower Assendon, the old turnpike road that is now the main road to Oxford from Henley rises into the hills to the small hamlet of Bix, high above the Warburg Nature Reserve in the nearby valley known as Bix Bottom. Here there is a derelict church of Saxon origin, known as Bix Brand which was abandoned in medieval times, although several graves are still visible. It seems likely that this was abandoned as the population in the lower valleys declined and a newer church was built at the top of the hill nearer to the main road. The search continues for another abandoned medieval church known as Bix Gibwyn. The Bix Bottom valley is very beautiful and quiet with excellent walking options, with the Oxfordshire Way and the paths in the nature reserve as well. The village today is split by the busy A4130, moreso as this is a dual carriageway where traffic is at speed. To the south is Bix Manor, a beautiful seventeenth century half-timbered house with walled gardens which is now a wedding venue and has a wonderful tithe barn that also hosts occasional art exhibitions. Nearby is the recently restored water pump and tanks, built in the Victorian era to refresh horses that had just climbed up from Henley. To the north is Bix Common, still an open area with public access and a small toll house has survived. Just at the western edge of the village a bridleway drops down into the woods, known as "the old Henley road". This track leads along a valley that is parallel to the modern road and leads towards Nettlebed through wonderful beech woods with mossy banks.

Nettlebed is the next village on the A4310 towards Wallingford. This was until recently a well serviced small town with its own butchers, grocers and other shops. The advent of the modern supermarkets in Henley within the past twenty years has forced changes and many of the former shops are now reverting to residential use. The good news is the initiative at the

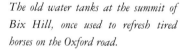

The old water tanks at the summit of Bix Hill, once used to refresh tired horses on the Oxford road.

old Church Hall that has created a new shop, post office and very good café. As we have seen in the northern Chilterns, where there are clay deposits brick making became a strong local industry and this is also the case at Nettlebed. The finest building is the old kiln that is now preserved just east of the village main street. Early photographs from around 1900 show just how important this industry was, with many pot kilns on Nettlebed Common and at nearby Crocker End. Windmill Hill was a heavily industrialised area by local standards, with dirt and smoke – a walk into this area, now wooded, still shows signs of hollows and pits where the clay was extracted and many other features that echo this period. Historic records indicate that all the tiles for Stonor House were made here, as well as the original materials for Wallingford Castle back in the fourteenth century. When it became popular to replace thatched roofs with tiles, the industry had a huge boom in demand. It is also interesting that contracts were made with people referred to as "Flemynge" in the context of being Flemish in origin. This is coincidental as the modern Flemings who have been linked to this village for generations were originally a jute trading family from Scotland. The modern Fleming family founded Flemings Bank in the City of London and provided us with the late Ian Fleming, and of course Bond, James Bond. There is also a strong thespian tradition in the family, which included Celia Johnson, famous for the leading role in *Brief*

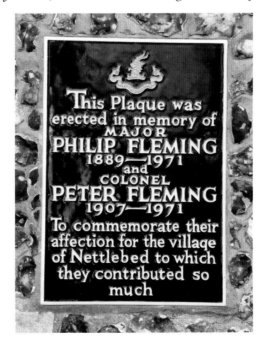

Far left: *One kiln has survived from the boom years and is now preserved at Nettlebed.*

Left: *The Fleming family have been associated with Nettlebed for generations.*

Encounter, Lucy Fleming and now Simon Williams. The Flemings still have an estate here although the historical home, Joyce Grove, has been a local hospice for many years. There is also an unusual cultural twist to Nettlebed, as the Village Club is the venue for one of the most popular jazz clubs, attracting well-known names to perform on Monday evenings throughout the year.

A short distance to the south is one of the most intimate properties owned by the National Trust. Greys Court is a small Tudor Manor with its own fortified tower in the grounds, with walled gardens and quiet corners. Only open to the public during the summer months, it represents a typical Chilterns scene, with views down the dry valley towards Henley and near to the local village of Rotherfield Greys. The gardens include vines and wisteria arches and there is a stone maze which is modern and great fun for children. There is also an unusual donkey wheel that was used to lift water from the deep well beside the house. The manor is named after a Norman knight, Anchetil de Greye, who was gifted the house. In Tudor times the Knollys family owned the house and Sir Francis Knollys was very close to Queen Elizabeth I as her Treasurer from 1572 until 1596. He was also tasked with the imprisonment of Mary Queen of Scots and is reputed to have formed a great respect for her during this period; the family were also closely connected to the Boleyn family. Unusually for this period

Greys Court, managed by the National Trust.

as a close advisor, he managed to keep his head and he and his wife are buried in an impressive tomb in nearby Rotherfield Greys church.

Close by is Greys Green. On a summer's day drivers should beware as the cricket ground is almost bisected by the road towards Peppard. A good batsman could make the boundary with the help of the bounce off a passing car. This summer scene is idyllic, with white flannels and a wooden pavilion, all flanked by converted barns and overlooked by a typical village hall, once used for a hilarious episode of *Jeeves and Wooster*. In spring, lines of cherry trees flank the approach to provide an early show of blossom to add to the scene.

From Greys there are several hamlets, Shepherds Green, Satwell and Highmoor, beside the main B481 that links Reading with Nettlebed and then Watlington. This area was used in 1944 to muster American forces prior to the D Day invasion in June. The woods provided excellent cover for the tanks and hundreds of vehicles to prevent detection by aerial reconnaissance. Cement roads were built through the woods and temporary camps set up. Locals can remember how this woodland city was literally abandoned overnight once the orders to move to the coast and disembark for France were issued. In addition to the roads which still survive, a curious model castle, made by the GI's during their long wait, still sits beside the B481 between Nettlebed and Highmoor. This was recently wiped out by a car accident, but has been happily restored and now remains as a lasting memorial to the many soldiers who were to lose their lives on Omaha Beach.

The small castle left by US forces preparing for D-Day in 1944.

These hamlets are typically blessed with lovely country houses and small pubs such as the Rising Sun at Witheridge Hill. Many Chiltern pubs are under pressure and have had to re-invent themselves more as restaurants, often with gourmet-trained chefs that need to attract clientele out of Henley and Reading. Perhaps one of the better known "gastro-pubs" is the Crooked Billet at Stoke Row. This was an old, run down pub before being purchased by Paul Clerehugh in the late 1980s and re-invented as one of the pioneers of really good food in a pub environment. He is now a nationally renowned celebrity chef and his restaurant has achieved many awards. It was a firm favourite for the late Sir John Mortimer and this is where Kate Winslet had her "first" wedding reception. The location is extraordinary, down a narrow lane that seems to decline in width and surface quality to the extent that anyone on their first visit would be forgiven for thinking that this must be a mistaken turn. Suddenly, this lane opens a little to reveal the most typical old Chiltern pub, with tables outside in summer and very un-typical food. Despite its success, it has managed to retain its earthy charm with rustic tables and collections of old framed photographs – it has its own definite style. Outside there are ancient bicycles and decaying old cars which have been consciously abandoned.

Stoke Row is another village at nearly 200 metres above sea level. It is almost entirely surrounded by beech woods and is particularly attractive during the bluebell and autumn periods. In the mid nineteenth century, a local squire from nearby Ipsden, Edward Anderdon

The Crooked Billet pub at Stoke Row.

Classic car wreck at the Crooked Billet.

Reade, had worked in India with the Maharaja of Benares. While there he was responsible for sinking a well in 1831 in Azimgurgh and had mentioned that water was also a problem in his own area back in England. In 1864, the Maharaja remembered this and returned the favour, gifting an elaborately designed well to the people of Stoke Row. This is one of the most exotic features of the Chilterns, with its cupola, elephants and Indian imagery. It is now quite a feature and much visited as a local curiosity. The well keeper's cottage is also intriguing as it must be one of the smallest dwellings locally, set in a lovely cherry orchard.

As with so many villages, working in the local woods to fashion the raw material for furniture making was the traditional way of life. The Second World War had an unusual impact here, as Stoke Row re-invented itself in the supply of tent pegs – in fact an estimated three million were made here as part of the war effort.

Almost within a stone's throw – across yet another dry valley – is Checkendon, another village with a very active cricketing tradition. The ground is in the heart of the village, opposite the village hall and overlooked by a beech wood. The nearby church is twelfth century in origin, built by monks from Bec in Normandy and well worth a visit, with a Laurence Whistler stained glass window. The churchyard is interesting as there are many Polish graves. In the Second World War a military camp was set up in the beech woods at

The Maharaja's Well at Stoke Row.

129

The remains of an old saw pit in the woods near Stoke Row.

Scots Common. Originally used by the RAF and then the USAF as a maintenance depot, it was used from 1948 as a re-settlement camp for Polish refugees who had fled to the Middle East and Africa. Not wishing to be repatriated to a doubtful future in post-war Poland, many hundreds lived in this village made of Nissen huts. Many settled in the area after finding work locally and older locals can still remember visiting the cinema at the camp as children. Today, the site remains but is now a timber yard. Checkendon was also the family home of Richard Burns, who was World Rally Champion in 2001 and sadly died from a rare form of brain tumour when only 34 years old; he is also buried in the churchyard.

Directly opposite the church are some half-timbered cottages, some of Tudor origin. Immediately adjacent to the church is Checkendon Court, a very fine listed Tudor country house with a long avenue of clipped yew hedges through manicured lawns. This is just one of the many country estates to be found in the area; another, Hook End Manor was once owned by David Gilmour of the Pink Floyd band and is still a recording studio today. Deep inside the woods, close to the old Polish camp at Scots Common, there is an extraordinary pub – the Black Horse. This has been owned by the Saunders family for many years and has resisted all the trends to modernise. Being a privately owned, the family could maintain control and uphold the old traditions, so a visit is rather like stepping back into the 1950s. The building

The Black Horse has remains a traditional country pub much favoured with locals.

The church at Checkendon with its Polish connections.

Tudor cottages at Checkendon.

The village sign at Checkendon depicts local scenes.

comprises a series of sitting rooms, with open fires in the winter, with local beer that was, until recently, still drawn from wooden barrels. The atmosphere is wonderful and the company usually local farmers discussing their next vintage tractor run in the summer months or walkers and cyclists stopping by. The modern trend of providing exotic meals has not been taken up here, although there is some basic food.

Moving south towards Reading, down the A4074, the settlements become distinctly more developed, with considerable post-war development of housing for commuters into Reading which is only a fifteen minute drive – and, of course, the train service to London. The "commons" theme continues, echoing the former role of these settlements as food providers for the nearby markets. The oddly named Gallowstree Common is the historic location for executions, named after on oak tree that used to stand away from other trees and was used, as its name implies, as a gallows. It is thought that the last hanging was in 1825 for sheep stealing. Close by is Kidmore End, with its original late eighteenth century well still surviving in the heart of its busy cross road next to the Victorian church. Now just a short distance from the boundary with Berkshire at Caversham, both of these settlements merge into the much larger Sonning Common, This should not be confused with Sonning-on-Thames, which is

about four miles to the east beside the Thames, although the name suggests that this was at one time a common ground for grazing that may well have supplied Sonning. Just north is Peppard Common, with the fine house used to film *Howards End* that sits at the edge of the common.

The final leg of this Chilterns discovery finishes with a return to the Thames. The hills continue to maintain height and then drop quite suddenly down to the river itself, as at Henley. To the south of Henley, after another dry valley with the hamlet of Harpsden, we come to Shiplake. For many, this word is associated with the school, Shiplake College, which sits alongside the river and has a fine rowing tradition. The opening of the branch line to Henley, with a stop at Shiplake, opened up a period of expansion with many houses built to service the demand from the increasing number of commuters. The village has a fine lock on the river, featured in Jerome K. Jerome's book *Three Men in a Boat*. It was also once the home of George Orwell, who is buried at Sutton Courtenay near Abingdon as Eric Blair.

The best way to experience the river here is to follow the Thames Path. The stretch from Shiplake to Sonning is very attractive, with small islands and wildfowl, twisting its way through an unspoilt landscape. Sonning Bridge is one of the oldest on the river – a brick arch bridge built in 1775, itself replacing a previous wooden bridge making this an important crossing point for trade in the Middle Ages. This is so narrow that it requires traffic lights as it can only accommodate the width of one vehicle, making this a notorious pinch-point during peak traffic periods. The Chilterns run down from Binfield Heath to Sonning Eye, on the Oxfordshire bank as the village itself is part of Berkshire and now very close to the urban sprawl of Reading. Close by the bridge is the Mill Theatre, a popular venue that offers dinner in addition to the show. It is very intimate, having been converted from the old watermill in 1982 after five years of work by the Richards family. The mill, dating back to at least the seventeenth century had fallen into disrepair having once been a major flour mill for Reading and even supplying London by river. Nearby is the French Horn, a prestigious hotel that specialises in gourmet food – once a coaching inn, it stands with gardens running down to the river in a beautiful setting, but take care of the occasional helicopter landings. Sonning Eye is also home to the newly formed Redgrave Pinsent Rowing Lake, formed from the old gravel pits beside the river. This was created to provide a straight stretch of water for training and events, as the Thames is unable to offer the usual 2000 metres of straight water. This can be clearly seen from the main line railway as one approaches Reading from London, on the opposite bank of the river.

The river soon reaches Reading, with Caversham on the Chiltern bank. As a major part of Reading, since 1911 the boundary for Berkshire here crosses the river and Caversham forms an urban outlier north of the river. This is very evident as Caversham is heavily developed and Oxfordshire is rural – there are few more distinctive boundaries than this when taking the

Opposite: *This house was used for the film* Howards End *starring Anthony Hopkins.*

Sonning Bridge is one the oldest on the Thames and is still only one lane width.

Opposite: *At Sonning.*

A4074 into Oxfordshire at Mapledurham. The hills are still very evident here, with a dry valley that has formed from several others to the north, with its terminus in the heart of the town centre. From Reading, once over the Caversham Bridge, all the roads immediately rise into quite steep hills, such as Priest Hill that becomes a problem in snow and icy conditions. Overlooking all of this, on the crest of the hill, is Caversham Park. This is now the headquarters of the BBC Monitoring Service, listening in on broadcasts from all over the world. Teams of international experts analyse the incoming reports and provide news analysis and information to the BBC and other news suppliers. The building is Victorian and occupies a site with a long history, having once been a castle after the Norman conquest, owned by Sir Francis Knollys in the Elizabethan era and later used to imprison Charles I. In order to support the BBC Monitoring activities the nearby Crowsley Park estate was also purchased and this is now the location for massive satellite dishes for the receiving station. As a consequence, the BBC is a large local employer and by its nature, very cosmopolitan. The nearby Caversham Heights is a prestigious locality for Reading's professional class.

From Caversham Bridge there are excellent boat cruises on the Thames in the summer months, on old Victorian style launches that were once powered by steam. These wonderful

boats provide outside seating for a fine view of the river all the way to Henley via the locks at Sonning and Shiplake. They finish beside the River and Rowing Museum at Mill Meadows and make for a good day out as one can return by train to Reading.

Immediately west of Caversham is a small lane, just behind St Peter's church called The Warren. This is part of an old terrace route – the Tuddingway – between Caversham and Wallingford that enabled the transport of goods down to Reading and subsequently to the inland ports and on to London. This track is still very evident and now forms the main path through Mapledurham and then forms part of the Thames Path from Whitchurch to Goring. This leads past some elegant riverside properties before turning into a track that leads to

Mapledurham House is one of the finest Elizabethan houses in the Chilterns.

Mapledurham. This is a good walk, but by car one needs to take the Woodcote road and follow the signs to drop back down a steep lane into this charming hamlet. Firmly back in rural Oxfordshire, rolling hills sweep down to the floodplain on the Thames and the parkland surrounding Mapledurham House and estate. This has been owned by the Eyston family, descendants of the Blount family since 1490, although the estate goes back to the Norman period. There are parallels with Stonor as this family managed to survive the Reformation period and maintain their Catholic heritage, explaining why the house has its own beautiful chapel even though it is next door to the charming parish church. There have been recent new discoveries of priest holes used to protect recusants, but the physical location provided a good place for sanctuary, with the river on one side and the fairly inaccessible hills clustered around the estate.

The Almshouses at Mapledurham, where the whole village is part of the estate.

Mapledurham is an enigma, as it is one of the finest Elizabethan houses in England, with the oldest surviving working watermill on the Thames, exquisite buildings including almshouses, a superb church and Elizabethan cottages. One grave in the churchyard is interesting as the tombstone records that the deceased, Sir Charles Rose MP, died "from the

The oldest watermill still operating on the Thames, at Mapledurham.

The weir at Mapledurham with the Chilterns in the background.

Opposite: *The largest river turbine in the UK at Mapledurham.*

The inner workings of the old watermill, still producing organic flour.

effects of an aeroplane flight" in 1913. Although visitors are increasing, this gem is still relatively unknown and deserves more profile, as it offers so much variety and high quality visits. Despite being so near Reading, its rural location is utterly peaceful. The estate is also a working farm with herds of dairy cattle to complete the pastoral scene and there are superb walks into the surrounding woods and to the river. It is rare example of a surviving, self-contained estate that supports a small community. It is also possible to stay here as there are holiday cottages to rent.

There is also a modern twist to the story of Mapledurham. The watermill, which is still working and producing organic flour, has now been carefully developed to house the UK's largest "Archimedes Screw" water turbine. This rests on the site of an older turbine that once fed the house with power, but this new development is the largest on the Thames and generates 100kwh into the national grid. The large water screw is visible and measures 3 metres across and is 8 metres long; the construction was a major undertaking, requiring the clearance of the old mill pond. Hopefully, this will be the first of many such turbines along the Thames Valley, totally carbon free and sustainable as long as the river flows.

Elizabethan country houses were popular in this area – as there is another one next door. Just a mile from Mapledurham, going west towards Whitchurch, is Hardwick House. This is reputed to be the setting for Kenneth Grahame's Toad Hall, with its sweeping lawns down to the river bank. The river here is such that it is easy to imagine Toad and Ratty getting up to their tricks along the banks. It is known that Charles I visited here – but as a prisoner under escort – and reputedly played bowls nearby at Collins End. Although not easy to reach by car, the bridleway along the valley between here and Mapledurham is a fine walk. Between Hardwick and Whitchurch-on-Thames the hills are high and steep, right down to the river

The view of the Chilterns plunging down to the Thames near Whitchurch.

Opposite: *The London train speeds its way over Gatehampton Bridge.*

The old iron bridge at Whitchurch is still a toll bridge.

floodplain. The best view of this is – surprisingly – from the fast trains between Bristol and London as they approach Reading. The view, especially in the early morning when the light is low, is stunning. The hills fold in shapes that are almost Tuscan in feel, topped by beech woods, offering a prospect of utterly unspoilt countryside, with the River Thames in the foreground. If the train is at its scheduled speed, within three minutes you would arrive at Reading station.

One of the last remaining toll bridges across the Thames is at Whitchurch, made of iron and built in 1902. In this village, again the Chilterns have an immediate impact, with the road rising to Whitchurch Hill being a serious climb, especially if the roads are wintry. It is linked to Pangbourne, on the opposite bank and in Berkshire. With a station at Pangbourne,

Looking towards Gatehampton Bridge near Goring in summer from Hartslock Reserve.

the village is highly attractive for commuters working in Reading and London, with Paddington being around 45 minutes on a good day. This has had the usual impact – as elsewhere throughout the Chilterns – on the local housing prices.

This exploration is now nearly at its end, as we complete the circle and return to Goring-on-Thames, the first location at the beginning of the first chapter. The Goring Gap is very evident as the Thames Valley narrows just north of Whitchurch and Pangbourne. The Thames Path takes a lovely route – again the Tuddingway – at high level above Coombe Park before dropping through steep woods with chalk outcrops to rejoin the river at Gatehampton near Goring. This is the location of one of the finest railway bridges across the Thames, where the Great Western line approached Goring. Built by Brunel in 1838, this brick bridge was so robust that it is still taking all the rail traffic on one of the busiest lines in the entire UK. Every few minutes there are high speed trains, freight trains and the slower Thames Valley link trains crossing the river.

It is therefore appropriate to complete this exploration with one final visit. One mile south of Goring is the nature reserve at Hartslock Woods, overlooking the Thames. This is run by the local Wildlife Trust (BBOWT) and is a famous site for its chalk grassland habitat and, in particular, the rare wild orchids in summer. The real gem of this place takes some effort – as you will need to walk to get to the reserve and then to take the path that climbs steeply up through the woods. It is well worth the exertion as the path emerges onto a small platform high above the valley below. The view is stunning. The railway line is clearly visible, with the perfect angle to see the curve of the River Thames and the railway bridge in the middle distance. Trains can be heard coming and there is always a moment of excitement as the train emerges onto the bridge and thunders through. It is a good place to end – a magnificent prospect across the Thames from a high point in the Chilterns, with the reminder of the continuous influence of communications on these beautiful hills.

LINKS FOR FUTURE REFERENCE

Aldbury Nowers Nature Reserv	www.hertswildlifetrust.org.uk/NatureReserves
Amersham	www.amersham.org.uk
Ashridge	www.nationaltrust.org.uk
Aston Rowant Nature Reserve	www.naturalengland.org.uk
Beaconsfield	www.beaconsfield.co.uk/townguide
Bekonscot Model Village	www.bekonscot.co.uk
Berkhamsted Castle	www.berkhamsted-castle.org.uk
Chalfont St Giles	www.chalfontstgiles.org.uk
Checkendon	www.checkendon.org
Chesham Museum	www.cheshammuseum.org.uk
Chiltern Brewery	www.chilternbrewery.co.uk
Chiltern Open Air Museum	www.coam.org.uk
Chiltern Valley Winery	www.chilternvalley.co.uk/winery
Chilterns Cycleway	www.chilternsaonb.org/cycleway
Chinnor and Princes Risborough Railway	www.chinnorrailway.co.uk
Ewelme	www.ewelme.info
Fox and Hounds, Christmas Common	www.foxandhoundschristmascommon.co.uk
Goring-on-Thames	www.goring-on-thames.co.uk
Grand Union Canal	www.canaljunction.com/canal/grand
Grangelands Nature Reserve	www.chilternsaonb.org
Great Missenden	www.great-missenden.co.uk
Greys Court	www.nationaltrust.org.uk/main/w-greyscourt
Hartslock Nature Reserve	www.hartslock.org.uk
Hellfire Caves	www.hellfirecaves.co.uk
Henley Royal Regatta	www.hrr.co.uk

Henley	www.visitsouthoxfordshire.co.uk/towns-villages/henley
High Wycombe	www.wycombe.gov.uk/tourism
HS2	www.hs2.org.uk
Hughenden Manor	www.nationaltrust.org.uk/main/w-hughendenmanor
Lacey Green Windmill	www.laceygreenwindmill.org.uk
Lardon Chase and The Holies	www.nationaltrail.co.uk
Living Chair Museum	www.stewartlinford.co.uk
Maharajah's Well	www.stokerow.net/well1.asp
Mapledurham	www.mapledurham.co.uk
Midsomer Murders	www.midsomermurders.org
Nettlebed	www.nettlebed.org.uk/nettlebed_history
Oxfordshire Way	www.oxfordshire.gov.uk/oxfordshireway
Pitstone Windmill	www.nationaltrust.org.uk/main/w-pitstonewindmill
Princes Risborough	www.princesrisborough.com
Roald Dahl Museum and Story Centre	www.roalddahlmuseum.org
Stokenchurch	www.stokenchurch.org.uk
Stonor House and Park	www.stonor.com
The Bull and Butcher at Turville	www.thebullandbutcher.com
The Chiltern Society	www.chilternsociety.org.uk
The Chilterns AONB	www.chilternsaonb.org
The Crooked Billet	www.thecrookedbillet.co.uk
The Icknield Way	www.icknieldwaypath.co.uk
The Lee	www.thelee.org.uk
The Ridgeway Long Distance Path	www.nationaltrail.co.uk/Ridgeway
Tring Natural History Museum	www.nhm.ac.uk/tring
Wallingford Castle	www.wallingfordmuseum.org.uk
Warburg Nature Reserve	www.bbowt.org.uk
Watlington Hill	www.ocv.org.uk/sites
Watlington	www.watlington.org
Wendover Woods	www.forestry.gov.uk/wendoverwoods
Wendover	www.wendover-pc.gov.uk
West Wycombe Park	www.nationaltrust.org.uk
Whitchurch	www.whitchurchonthames.com
William Penn	www.quakerinfo.com/quakpenn.shtml
Woodcote	www.woodcote-online.co.uk
Wormsley Cricket Ground	www.wormsleycricket.co.uk